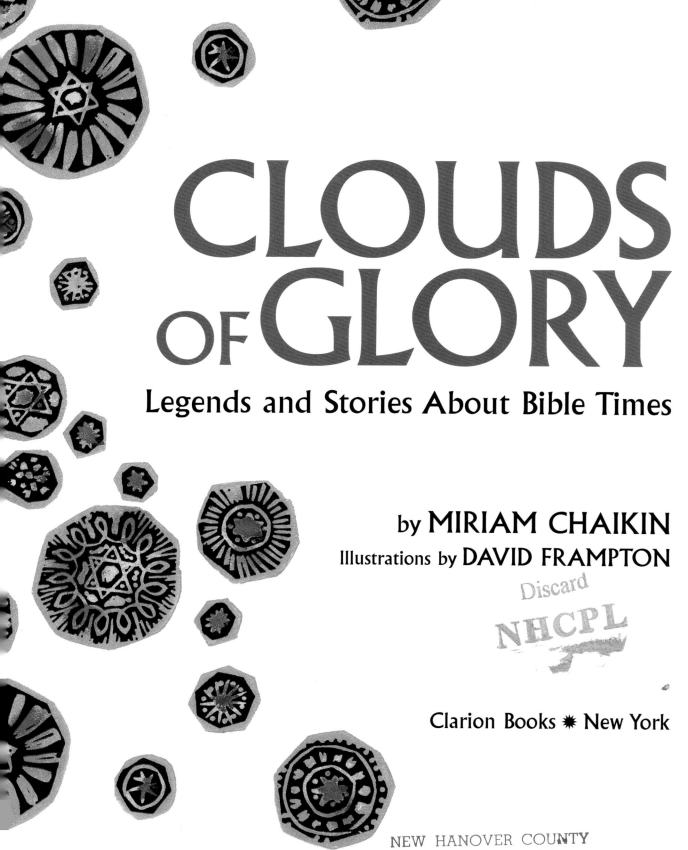

CLOUDS OF GLORY

Legends and Stories About Bible Times

by **MIRIAM CHAIKIN**

Illustrations by **DAVID FRAMPTON**

Clarion Books ✳ New York

Clarion Books
a Houghton Mifflin Company imprint
215 Park Avenue South, New York, NY 10003

The text is set in 14/20-point Dante.
The illustrations were executed in woodcut.

Printed in Singapore

For information about permission
to reproduce selections from this book,
write to Permissions, Houghton Mifflin Company,
215 Park Avenue South, New York, NY 10003.

Library of Congress Cataloging-in-Publication Data
Clouds of glory : legends and stories about Bible times / Miriam Chaikin
p.   cm
"The stories in this book are largely based on Rashi's commentary on the book Genesis, and on
midrashic threads found in Louis Ginsbergs's Legends of the Bible and in Raphael Patai's
Gates to the Old City"—Acknowledgments.
Summary: Presents twenty-one stories, in a single narrative, about God's relationship with His creation,
from creating angels on the second day to testing Abraham's love.
ISBN 0-395-74654-X
1. Legends, Jewish. 2. Bible stories—O. T. Genesis. 3. Midrash—Juvenile literature. [1. Midrash.
2. Bible stories—O. T. 3. Jews—Folklore.] I. Rashi, 1040-1105. Perush Rashi ' al ha–Torah.
II. Ginzberg, Louis, 1873-1953. Legends of the Bible.   III. Gates to the Old City.   IV. Title.
BM530.C48 1997
296.1´9—dc21   97-5042
                                                                          CIP
                                                                          AC
TWP   10   9   8   7   6   5   4   3   2   1

In memory of Merlin
Kishinev, 1910– New York, 1994
—M. C.

The stories in this book are largely based on Rashi's commentary on the Book of Genesis, and on Midrashic threads found in Louis Ginzberg's *Legends of the Bible* and in Raphael Patai's *Gates to the Old City, A Book of Jewish Legends*.

*As a pearl results from an irritant
in the shell of an oyster,
so may legends arise from an irritant
in Scripture.*

Shalom Spiegel's introduction
to Louis Ginzberg's single-volume *Legends of the Bible*.

CONTENTS

INTRODUCTION

There is a vast body of Jewish literature that is little known even among Jews. It is called Midrash. The Hebrew word means "search and explain." Ancient rabbis, who originated the Midrash stories, believed that the Bible held the answer to all questions. "Turn it and turn it," they said of the Bible's pages. "For everything is in it." When something in the Bible puzzled them, they searched its pages for an answer.

The explanation they found is a Midrash—Midrashim in the plural.

The rabbis used Midrashim to teach the Bible and to enliven their sermons. They wove in folktale motifs and other story elements. They added to existing Midrashim, creating new ones. And the body of literature known as Midrash grew and grew.

A sample midrash concerns the story of Creation. The Bible tells that God made seas, heavens, lands, trees, plants, and animals. Someone wondered: "How did God make the heavens?"

The rabbis would have answered that this was not a human concern, that the secrets of heaven belong to God. All the same, they would have quoted the prophet Isaiah: "He stretched out the heavens as a curtain, and spread them out as a tent."

This answer is a Midrash.

Another question came up about God's saying, "Come, let us make humans in our image."

Who was God talking to when he said "us"? He had created only seas, heavens, lands, trees, plants, and creatures. There were no people.

One Midrash says, "God was talking to these, the things he had created."

Another came about this way: True, angels are not listed. Yet angels appear in Bible stories. Jews sing about angels on the Sabbath. They mention angels in their prayers. This tells us that not everything that was created was listed. The Midrash? God was talking to the angels.

To qualify as a Midrash, a story must answer a question that the Bible raises, and it must be based on Bible teachings:

God created the universe and all life.

God created a wonderful world for people to enjoy.

God is goodness and wants us to be like him.

What is *goodness*? That question also generated many Midrashim:

Goodness is loving kindness.

Love your neighbor as yourself.

Do not do to others what you would not want them to do to you.

Be thoughtful of the stranger, eyes for the blind, feet to the lame, caretakers of the poor.

Loving kindness should extend to animals as well.

Where is God? The Midrashim that came to answer the question created a heavenly kingdom. And the prophets, who had visions of the kingdom, supplied imaginative details. The prophet Isaiah said, "Heaven is my throne and the earth my footstool." The prophet Ezekiel described it as being "full of the brightness of the Lord's glory." And high up, " . . . over the heads of angels, there appeared . . . a sapphire stone in the likeness of a throne."

Through Midrash angels became heaven's inhabitants. Midrash and prophets and commentators assigned them characteristics. The prophet Ezekiel said they had "feet like the sole of a calf's foot, and they sparkled like the color of burnished brass," and that they had "human hands under their wings."

They were said to have wisdom and power and to be able to turn themselves into any shape—the wind, a bee, a human. Their power, however, is limited. They are God's servants and can do only what he tells them to do.

A Midrash is something like an angel. It, too, may be any shape, from a single word, to a saying, to a story. It may be a fantasy, a Midrash with wings. But its power is also limited. It must serve a principle that the Bible teaches.

The stories in this book are woven of Midrash and legend. Chapter titles are Midrashim. The stories range from Creation to the binding of Isaac. Appearing in them, side by side with Bible characters, are angels; the Great Heavenly Choir; the Shekina, God's female earth presence; and that rogue, Satan.

In this book, angels Raziel and Michael are treated as females. This Midrash, the author's own, is based on the Midrash, "God was talking to the angels when he said, 'Come, let us make humans in our image.'" The humans that resulted from the work were male and female. This Midrash tells us that there were male and female models in heaven.

These stories obey the laws of Midrash: They are based on Bible teachings and are faithful to the sense of the original verse. The words of the prophet Jeremiah allow for a new interpretation. He likened the word of God to "a hammer that breaks the rock in pieces." As a rock can be broken into many pieces, so can a single verse have many meanings. Sarah's story is based on the words of the Bible commentator Rashi that "Sarah was a Seer."

God created the angels to be his helpers and companions.

CHAPTER 1
God Created the Angels on the Second Day

No leaf was there, no bone, no shape, nor color. Heard only was a quiet slosh made by dark waters. Always and always, the same dark waters. Always and always, the same slosh. God wearied of the sight, separated the waters, and began to make a world. He created thing after thing, keeping what he liked, and discarding what he did not like.

When he finished, he had made a world full of wonders—a blue sky above, seas below, with lands between them and each place full of living, breathing creatures. The creatures appealed to him, and he made them male and female, so they would reproduce themselves and live forever. And he covered the face of the earth and the floor of the sea with plant food for all. And he put lights in the sky to give the world shades of light and darkness. The comings and goings of the light made a day in the world.

This day lasted from sunset to sunset. But God's day was a thousand years. And all the things he made, the world and everything in it, he made in five of his days.

He glanced over the world, inspecting each detail. The angels did the same. So full of wonders was the world, so covered with marvels, the talkative angels fell silent before its beauty.

Who were these angels?

They were airy beings that God had made for himself as helpers and companions. For the world with the blue sky was not the only world he had made. Above it, he had made a second world for himself and his angels. It was made of seven heavens strung together, one above the other. In each, a million million angels of one kind or another hovered or flew about.

Most angels had six wings, three on each side, and hands beneath the wings. They had calves' feet, but angels' feet were golden in color. They were God's servants, and whatever God told them to do, they did. They could change their shapes to carry out the task assigned to them and become a wind, a gnat, a donkey. Wheel and Flame Angels kept their shapes. So did the Adorers, Rain Bringers, Wind Throwers, Arguers, Past and Future Knowers, Plant and Sorcery Knowers, and all the other specialist angels.

The Great Heaven, as the angels called the seven heavens together, was vast. So vast, that each heaven could hold many more millions of angels and still be roomy. So vast, that if all angels stretched out their wings at the same time, no two wingtips would come near each other. Heaven was so vast, an earth creature would have to walk for five hundred years to cross it from side to side, and another five hundred years to cross it going up or down.

And God, where was he? He was in the seventh heaven, the highest heaven, hidden by a white garment. The angels called this garment the Holy Curtain. No angel could see God. Not the archangels and their legions in the seventh heaven, not the singers and musicians who made up the great Heavenly Choir, not the specialist angels who came and went. Not even Raziel, who sat outside the Holy Curtain and could hear God's breath, not even she could see him.

But all angels could see his Glory, for the amber glow that radiated out from the Holy Curtain touched every angel in every heaven. This was the source of their happiness. For this they yearned when they had to leave Heaven. Their chief joy, their only joy, their sweetest joy was the touch of Glory.

Angels who went from heaven to heaven used all six wings to fly. But while in the seventh heaven, they used only two. Angel Raziel, who was fond of ceremonies, had introduced the custom.

"The Heavenly Choir sings love songs to the Creator," she had said to the angels. "Let us show our love with signs."

"What are signs?" asked an angel.

"They stand for words," Raziel had said. "With two wings, let us cover our face, to say that even a small measure of Glory is enough for us. With two, let us cover our feet, to show our gladness that heaven, not earth, is our place."

Raziel noticed a shift in the amber rays at the Holy Curtain. "Sh-sh," she said. Using one of the names by which angels called God, she added, "The Holy One is again inspecting his world."

The angels were not surprised. He had made world after world, trying to create one he liked. This one, under the blue sky, he liked and kept. Yet he continued to inspect its details and working parts, improving this, discarding that.

Raziel and the angels saw that his gaze rested on the sea, with its many levels, and with different fish occupying each level.

"The sea is very deep," the Holy One said.

"Oh yes," the angels answered. They knew how deep it was. They had seen a bird flying over the sea carrying a stone between its feet. The bird dropped the stone, and it fell for seven years before reaching bottom.

"I will make Leviathan, a great fish, as a plaything for myself, and as a monitor of the deep," he said.

The angels loved it when the Holy One created something new. They watched the waters churn and heave and saw an enormous, shimmering creature rise briefly to the surface and disappear again. They marveled at the sight.

"Only one, beloved?" Raziel said. "Where is its mate? All the creatures you made, you made in pairs, male and female."

"There will be no mate for Leviathan," the Holy One said. "If there were two and they had children, they would drink up the seas and destroy my world."

The angels, humming agreement, saw the wisdom of it.

The Holy One made two more invisible peacekeepers: Ziz, a gigantic bird with an enormous wingspan, and Behemoth, a great and noble land creature, whose roar alone could keep peace among the beasts.

The Holy One once more glanced over his world. "It is better, " he said.

When their beloved was pleased, the angels were in raptures. The very air of heaven danced with joy.

"Singers! Musicians!" Raziel called to the Heavenly Choir. "A song of praise for the great works that the Holy One has made!"

Seven hundred thousand male voices and a like number of female voices burst into song. A hundred thousand angel musicians, making harp and bell-like sounds with their lips, accompanied the singers as they sang, "He made the world in five days, in five days he made it. Oh—the wonder of it all! The wonder of it all! His glorious fingerprints are everywhere!"

The male chorus sang alone, "With wisdom he made his world. The moon and stars, the streams and brooks, he made them, we saw it."

The female chorus sang, "Who causes grass to spring up for the cattle? Who opens his hand, and feeds all his creatures? Who is God in heaven above and on earth below?"

All voices sang together, "God is God in Heaven above and on earth below. He was, he is, he will ever be."

CHAPTER 2
The Angels Are Jealous

The angels loved to watch the world below. They liked the different shapes and movements. They especially liked watching the arrival of night and day. In heaven, it was always light. On the sixth day, as they watched the sun roll across the face of the earth casting light on dark places, they heard the Holy One say, "I have made a good world, but something is missing."

The words surprised them. They had thought the world was finished. But they had no say in what the Holy One did and did not do, so they said nothing.

Raziel spoke for them, saying, "It is your world, Holy One, to do with as you please."

The angels quickly accepted the idea of a new creature and began to shimmer with curiosity. Each thing the Holy One had created was greater than the one before. What marvel would he create this time?

One angel, the archangel Satan, was less accepting of the idea. He liked things as they were. Angels were the highest form of creation and first in the Holy One's affections. A new creature could change that.

The Arguer Angels began raising a fuss. "What can be missing, Holy One?" they said. "You planned every detail. You made each thing not once, not twice, but again and again. Your world is perfect. Everything is in it."

"The Arguers again!" angel Raziel thought. She wished the Holy One weren't so patient with them and thought he should silence them. Instead, he engaged them in conversation.

"Not everything," he said. "It needs one more creature."

"The world is full of creatures," the Arguers said. "The variety amazes—they walk, they leap, they creep and crawl, they swim through the waters and fly in the air."

Satan waited to hear the Holy One's response.

"One more is needed," he said.

"But why?" asked the Arguers. "We can change ourselves into anything—fire, water, wind, a gnat, an elephant. As one thing or the other we can do anything."

"Can you take care of the earth?" the Holy One said.

The Arguers fell silent. They could not do that. No angel could. An angel was a creature of heaven.

Satan had thought the new creature would be a new group of stars, or a new type of beast or bird. He saw now that he had been wrong. He could no longer leave questions to the Arguers. They were too easily aroused and too easily silenced.

"Holy One," he said. "Of all the earth creatures you have made, is there not one who can take care of the earth?"

"Can the wild ox prune a tree? The ostrich lays her eggs on the ground where animals trample them. Does she have sense enough to do it?" said the Holy One.

Satan's fears were rising. "Then the new creature will be a beast with sense?" he said, hopefully.

"Not a beast, a human," said the Holy One. "A creature more like ourselves, made in our image."

Satan's hopes were dashed. He could say no more. He did not have to. The Arguers had found their voices again.

"Holy One," they said. "We are that creature! You made us with your breath and in your image!"

Raziel wished she could be more patient, like the Holy One, but the Arguers made that difficult. With an angry flap of her wings, she said, "Oh, you fools in heaven! He made us in his image, but are we like him? Can we create life? Can we dry up rivers, command the winds, shrivel mountains? We live forever, in that way we are like him. But in nothing else."

The Holy One saw the discomfort of the Arguers and set them at ease.

"My children," he said. "Everything I made is wonderful. Some things are more wonderful than others. The stars are superior to the sky because they give light. Trees are superior to stars because they give food. Beasts find their own food and shelter and are superior to stars. The new creature will have understanding and speech and will be superior to the beasts. But they will not be superior to you. You, my heavenly children, are my eternal companions and my greatest creation."

The Arguer Angels beamed and sparkled with pleasure. Even Satan was comforted. But Raziel was suddenly agitated. The angels had overlooked something. They had become so caught up in the Arguers' prattle that they had forgotten to think of the Holy One. She made a ceremony of what she had to say.

"Angels! Do we have a source of pleasure?" she called.

The angels, knowing her fondness for ceremonies, joined in. "We have one source of pleasure and only one," they answered.

"What is that?"

"Our greatest joy, our chief joy, our only joy is to be near the Holy One."

"And the Holy One, what is his source of pleasure?"

The angels hesitated. No one seemed to know. A small voice in the Heavenly Choir asked, softly, "Our songs of praise?"

"In heaven, yes, but who is there on earth to praise him?" Raziel said. "Does the lion marvel at the order in the night sky? Does the antelope stand back to admire a tree? The cat, is it moved by the beauty of a flower?"

"They cannot, they do not have understanding for it," said a scattering of angel voices.

"Just so," said Raziel. "The new creature will have understanding. And will notice beauty. And will marvel at the wonders of the world. And, moved by feelings of love, will sing songs of praise to the Holy One. He, too, will then have a source of pleasure."

The idea of a singing creature left Satan cold. But the Arguers were beside themselves with embarrassment for their selfishness in thinking only of themselves.

"Come, my children," said the Holy One. "Let us make humans in our image, after our likeness."

A burst of angel laughter tinkled through heaven.

Raziel explained the laughter. "Holy One," she said. "You are kind to say that. You made the world without our help and do not need our help for this, either."

"You will see that I do," the Holy One said. Stationed around the Holy Curtain, with their legions behind them, were the archangels Michael, Gabriel, Uriel, and Raphael. He called them by name and said, "Go down and bring me earth from the four corners of the world."

With four strokes of their wings the archangels went down, and with four more they returned, each carrying earth of a different color—red, black, yellow, and white. The Holy One took the earth, mixed it with water, and began to mold two forms.

"They will be made of clay, the new singing creatures," Satan muttered to himself with growing contempt.

There was a great stir in heaven as angels came from all directions to see what the Holy One would make.

"Holy One," said an angel, watching two forms being shaped. "Why do you use earth from the four corners of the world?"

"And why the different colors?" said another.

"To prevent future quarrels," the Holy One said. "These two will be the first parents and the ancestors of all humans. Their descendants will not be able to say, '*I am from the south, like the first parents.*' Or, '*I am red, like the first parents.*'"

Raziel felt a rush of love for the Holy One. "Heart's Delight," she said. "Great and deep is your wisdom."

The Heavenly Chorus took her words and made a song of them. With musician angels making harplike sounds with their lips, thousands of male and female voices sang, "Great and deep is his wisdom, how great it is. Great and deep is his wisdom, how very great it is. O great and deep is his wisdom."

Five hours later, the two humans were finished. As they lay stretched out on the ground. The Holy One added a soul to each. Then he took a measure of goodness from himself and added that as well. He paused before proceeding. He had made the humans good, because he wanted them to be good. But was it goodness if he himself had made them good? If they could be no other way? If they had no choice?

No. Goodness had to be a matter of choice.

The angels hovering over the two forms on the ground were too enchanted with the new creatures to notice anything. But Satan had been watching and had seen the Holy One slip into the corner of each human heart an evil urge.

The humans would have two urges, one to do good, one to do evil. The choice would be theirs. The evil urge looked innocent enough, being tiny, slim as a spider hair, and asleep. But when aroused, it could swell greatly and smother a good intention. Satan would make use of the thing, though in what way he did not yet know.

The Holy One breathed his breath into the nostrils of the humans, giving them life, and stood them up on their feet.

"His name is Adam, Earth," he said. "Hers is Eve, Birth."

Raziel and the angels could not take their eyes from the splendid humans.

"Already they show understanding," Raziel said, watching Adam and Eve glance about themselves, forming with their lips the words—*sky, earth, beasts, trees.*

The Holy One took from himself two wisps of Glory and placed one wisp around the man and the other around the woman.

This was too much for Satan to bear. "Holy One," he said. "Your greatest gift you bestow on two lumps of clay?"

"They will be my partners," the Holy One said. "I made a good world. They can make it better."

"These lumps, who are only a few hours old? Who know nothing?" Satan said.

"They will learn and I will help them," said the Holy One.

"They might refuse to be your partners," Satan said. "Why take the chance? Order them to make the world better."

"I want them to want to do it," the Holy One said. "Then I will know they love me."

"Order them to love you," Satan said. The Holy One sighed.

"I can do everything but that," he said. "I can create life and end it, turn mountains into dust. But I cannot make humans love me."

Stretched out on the earth was a secret corner of heaven called the Garden of Eden. He took the two humans and put them there to live. Every fruit-giving tree grew in the garden, every plant, every sweet-smelling herb. A river ran through it, nourishing it with water.

"Have children, and fill my world with people," the Holy One said to Adam and Eve.

To the angels, he said, "Love my humans."

"Oh, Heart's Delight, we do, we do," they answered.

Satan's voice was missing from the chorus.

"Love them?" he said to himself. "I see no reason even to like them."

CHAPTER 3
Satan Is Cast Out of Heaven

Satan was eaten up by jealousy. He made no effort to hide his feelings and openly went from heaven to heaven trying to stir up the angels and set them against the humans. He claimed the humans were common, that they were a low form of creation, that they were talking beasts on two legs. "They are made of dust," he said. "Can such a creature be worthy of the Holy One's love?"

And he always ended with, "My concern is for the Holy One. I don't want him to be disappointed."

The angels fled when they saw Satan approaching. If they could not get away in time, they stopped up their ears as he spoke.

The Holy One watched but did nothing.

"You are too patient with him, beloved," Raziel said.

The archangels agreed.

"Already, he has won over some of the lesser angels," said Michael.

"It will pass," said the Holy One.

"He is polluting heaven," said Gabriel.

"He is creating sour currents," said Uriel.

"Bitterness is contagious," said Raphael.

When it did not pass, and did not pass, the Holy One said to Satan, "You have soiled my sacred precincts. Heaven is not your place. I banish you and your followers from these holy corridors forever!"

The Casting-Out Gates of heaven opened and Satan and his followers went tumbling down.

"The Holy One will yet see that he has made a mistake in creating the humans," Satan told himself as he fell.

The angels were transformed as they fell. The amber glow that had surrounded them disappeared. Their iridescent wings became dull and colorless, and the three on each side became one. Their feet, which had been golden, turned brown. And they sprouted tails.

They would remain angels. And they would live forever and retain angel knowledge. But they would be a despised class of angels. They would be in disgrace. And when they stopped falling where did they land? On Mount Hermon—the mount of banishment—a desolate place, where they had for company only jackals, scorpions, strong winds, and one another.

Satan banished to Mount Hermon.

CHAPTER 4
What Does the World Yet Lack? Only Rest

When Satan left heaven, every last sour current left with him and once more sweet songs were heard and harmony and order and gentle feelings prevailed. The angels, busy with their duties again, were so captivated by the Holy One's new creation that they kept stealing glances at the garden to look at them.

Adam and Eve walked hand in hand in the twilight, looking and looking, and delighting in all they saw. The path under their feet was paved with rubies, lapis, and emeralds, and flecked with gold. On one side of them were apple orchards and pomegranate groves. On the other were figs and other fruit-giving trees and grapevines. Flowering shrubs and sweet-smelling herbs grew everywhere.

Everything in the garden was lovely and dear, but the aromas—oh, the aromas!

"Smell, Adam," Eve said, inhaling the sweet scent of jasmine that a breeze brought their way.

Adam did so and caught a whiff of honeysuckle. "Here's another," he said, inhaling deeply.

They were in raptures over the sweet smells. To catch them—the better to savor them—they closed their eyes and stood inhaling, inhaling, and making noises of

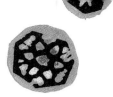

gladness. When they opened their eyes again, night had fallen and they were surrounded by darkness. Alarm seized them.

"Adam," Eve said. "The light, where is it?"

Adam darted about in the darkness looking for the light. "It is gone," he said.

Confused, trembling with fright, they held each other, afraid to move, even to speak.

The Holy One felt sorry for them. "Michael," he said to the archangel. "They are new in the world and know nothing. Send down two of your angels to teach them."

"I like the humans, Holy One," Michael said. "May I go?"

"You may," said the Holy One.

With four flaps of her wings she flew down to the garden and turned herself into a silky breeze. Floating over to Adam and Eve, she played gently over them, warming them, soothing them with her touch, and singing softly, *"Ei-lu-lu, Ei-lu-lu,"* to comfort them.

The trembling left Adam and Eve. They felt safe again.

"I am Michael, the messenger of God," Michael said. "God has sent me to teach you about the day. He has made it with two faces, one light, one dark. One comes, the other goes, the other comes again. So he has ordered the day to be. Fear not. The light will come again."

She took two flint stones from under her wing, struck them together, and produced two little flames. "This is fire," she said. "It can help or destroy. Use it well."

Not of her doing, but because it was time for them to appear in the sky, three stars twinkled and glittered overhead. A cloud that had covered the moon sailed on, and the moon came into view. There was light in the garden again. Adam and Eve saw the outlines of trees and bushes and the shining eyes of garden creatures.

"The daylight we saw was brighter," Adam said.

"This light belongs to the night," the angel said. "The stars mark the days. When they appear, a new day starts. The seventh day has just begun. The light you saw earlier, that will come again."

She could not bear to be away from the Holy One for long. Yearning to be near Glory again, she lifted off, with her angel wings sounding softly as she went.

In the garden, leaves rustled, animal feet scurried up trees and between bushes, an owl hooted, and Adam and Eve felt their entire beings filling with gladness. They sank to their knees and in an outpouring of love for God sang, "Great God who rolls away the day and brings on the night, who made us and surrounded us with marvels and wonders, we cannot see you, but your glorious fingerprints are everywhere."

In heaven, the angels knew from the sparkle in the amber glow that the Holy One was pleased.

"What did I tell you?" Raziel said. "The humans are not yet a day old and already they praise God."

"My work is over," said the Holy One. "Now I shall rest."

"Angels!" Raziel called, initiating a ceremony. "The Holy One declares a Sabbath, a day of rest."

The angels did their part. "A Sabbath, a day of rest," they repeated.

"Does the Holy One grow weary?" Raziel asked.

"He does not."

"Does he tire?"

"He does not."

"Then why does he rest?"

"To rejoice in the great work he has made."

"Shall he rejoice alone?" Raziel said.

"No."

"What do we do?"

"Keep him company," the angels chanted. "Rest and rejoice with him."

The very air crackled with joy.

"Singers, musicians!" Raziel called. "A psalm, a song for the Sabbath."

Heaven rang with sweet sound as the musician angels made a harp melody with their lips to accompany the choir's singing, "How great are your deeds, Beloved. Your works make us glad."

Raziel flew to the place where heaven and earth meet for a kiss, and called down, "Let everything that has breath rejoice!"

The earth responded.

"A song for God!" crowed the rooster.

The land hummed, the seas roared, trees danced, cattle lowed, horses neighed, frogs croaked, crickets chirped, birds made sweet sounds, each thing sang in its own voice, saying, "God is, God was, God ever will be."

"Now all creation together!" Raziel cried.

The voices of all creation came together, singing, "Holy, Holy, Holy is God, the whole world is full of his Glory. He is our beloved and we are his."

CHAPTER 5
The Shekina, God's Female Side and His Earth Presence

Adam and Eve were awakened by the chirping of birds. They listened for a while to the sweet sounds, then turned to watch the sun roll across the face of the earth, throwing light as it went. A happy, gurgling noise came to their ears. The sound gladdened their hearts.

"Come, let us go find it," Adam said.

They rose and followed the sound, listening, determined not to lose it. Then they came to the source, a fast-running brook, skipping over stones, and hurrying through the garden. Delighted with their find, they walked along with the brook, going where it went, curious about the animals they met along the way, and stopping to marvel over them.

The animals, just as curious, stopped to examine them.

"Look, Adam," Eve said. "Their eyes are like ours."

Adam looked and saw that it was so.

"What are they called?" Eve said.

"They have no names," Adam said.

"Then let us name them," Eve said.

A large bird with a slow step and colorful tail passed in front of them, giving them a sidelong glance.

"Peacock," Adam said, naming the bird.

"Monkey," Eve said of the furry creature that swung down on a branch for a closer look at them.

A thick, large four-legged beast with horns appeared.

"What name?" Eve said.

"Ox."

"And that one there, with its face to the trees?"

"Donkey," said Adam.

The animals also noticed similarities between themselves and the humans—and differences as well. The humans had no tail. And the thin amber cloud that covered each one—what was it?

But two pairs of eyes, both unfriendly, had also been following Adam and Eve. One pair belonged to Serpent, an animal who stood on two feet and was as tall as a camel. "King of the Garden," the other animals called him. Serpent had sensed the presence of strangers in his garden and gone to look for them. He had been hiding behind trees and following Adam and Eve ever since. Who were they? Why were they there?

The second pair of eyes, which watched Adam and Eve from high above the garden, belonged to Satan. An angel in disgrace could not set foot in the garden. The closest he could come to it was to fly one parasang, about three and one third miles, above the tallest tree. Forced to fly above the garden, Satan could not reach Adam and Eve to work his mischief on them. And what was that? To stir up the evil urge in them, make them do something to displease God.

When Satan noticed Serpent following the humans, he said to himself, "Serpent will do for me what I am unable to do for myself." And as Serpent stood inspecting the amber cloud around the humans, wondering what it was for, Satan acted. He placed on a passing breeze headed for the garden the words, "The amber cloud is a wisp of glory, a mark of God's love."

The words arrived in Serpent's ear and enraged him.

A silence fell on the garden, and the voice of God said, "Adam and Eve, I make you masters over this Garden and over the beasts. Take care of both."

"They will not be my masters," Serpent thought.

"May we eat whatever grows here?" Adam said.

"Every fruit, every dainty is yours," said the voice.

"Fruits and dainties that used to be mine!" Serpent said to himself, fuming.

"Except one," the voice continued. "The tree beside you is mine. Do not eat its fruit. Do not touch the tree or you will die."

No more was said. The voice stopped speaking.

Adam took a handful of grapes to eat and went to sit at the edge of the brook to watch the rushing waters.

But Eve, Eve could not move from the spot. God's tree had captivated her. She could not take her eyes from the color and form of the beautiful fruit that hung in abundance from every branch.

As Serpent, fuming, stood watching her, Satan again came to his aid. A passing breeze said to him, "Get her to eat the forbidden fruit. She will get him to eat it. God will be angry, take the garden away from them, and give it back to you."

Pleased with the idea, and with himself for thinking of it, Serpent strode out from behind the tree, went up to Eve, and said, "Did God say you would die if you ate the fruit of any tree?"

"Oh, not any tree," Eve said. "Just this one."

"This one?" Serpent said, leaning on the tree.

"Don't—" Eve gasped.

Serpent laughed. "Why not?" he said. "Nothing happened."

Eve stared wide-eyed as Serpent reached up with his neck and bit off a fruit.

"You will die," she said. "God said so—"

"Did I die?" he said, eating and smacking his lips with enjoyment. "Besides, God didn't mean you as a person would die. He was talking about the cloud around your body. He meant it would die. But what do you need it for? I don't have it. The other creatures don't."

Eve glanced about and saw that it was so.

Satan watched the progress of the conversation from above.

As Serpent ate, crunching and making noises of enjoyment, Eve's mouth began to water. She glanced up at the tree, so full of fruit. With the lowest branch just over her head, she could easily reach up and take one. But God had said not to, and she would not.

"Do you know why God told you not to eat that fruit?" Serpent said.

"God doesn't owe me any explanations," Eve said. "The world is his. He made it."

"He made it, but how did he know what to do?" Serpent said.

Eve had no answer.

"This tree gives knowledge," Serpent said. "Whoever eats its fruit knows everything. God ate a fruit and learned how to make the world. He told you and Adam not to eat the fruit because he doesn't want you to know as much as he does."

Eve did not know what to think. But one thing was clear. Serpent ate the fruit and did not die. And if the fruit does give knowledge, then Serpent knows everything. What he says must be so.

Serpent took another bite. "Umm, delicious," he said. "Go ahead, take one."

Eve wanted to. Oh, how she wanted to.

"Are you afraid God will be angry with you?" Serpent said, chewing.

Eve nodded.

"Don't be," Serpent said. "God rarely gets angry. And when he does, it doesn't last long. All you have to do is cry a little and say you're sorry. He'll forgive you and love you as before."

Satan, seeing that his protégé no longer needed his help, returned to Mount Hermon.

Eve's hand flew up. She snatched a fruit, then snatched another. "One for Adam," she said going to him.

"Adam," she said, "here is a fruit from—"

"Don't name it," he said, recognizing the fruit. If he heard the name, he would have to refuse the fruit. He took it eagerly and they both ate. And so delicious was the taste, they failed to notice the amber cloud around them growing thinner and thinner until it disappeared altogether. When they looked they saw that they were naked.

The sight embarrassed them. Eve took a handful of broad leaves from the fig tree and wove two aprons, one for herself and one for Adam.

Heaven grew momentarily darker.

"I am sorry I made them," the Holy One said with a sigh.

The angels could have cried for him. The humans were not yet a day old. And already they had disappointed him.

Raziel tried to cheer up the Holy One. "It was a good intention, Holy One," she said.

Archangel Gabriel agreed and also spoke comforting words. He then went on to speak of justice. "You warned them, Holy One," he said. "You told them they would die, and they must die. That would be right and just."

"Just, yes, but not right," the Holy One said. "They are new in the world and have not yet learned much. How can I let them die? No, this alters my view of justice. I see that justice and mercy are like two eyes. They cannot be separated."

Raziel felt an intense rush of love for the Holy One. "Oh, beloved," she said. "How deep are your thoughts, how precious."

"Amen and amen," came the sweet bell-like voices of the angels.

Only the Arguer Angels found something to complain about. "Holy One," they said. "We see mercy, but where is the justice? Are you not going to punish them?"

"If I do not punish them, future generations will not believe me," the Holy One said. "I am going down to banish them from the garden."

Now the Holy One does not go down. He does not leave heaven. It is the Shekina, his earth presence, who goes. When God is seen on earth, it is she who is seen. When God's voice is heard, it is the Shekina speaking.

The Shekina separated herself from the whole of Glory and went down.

Adam and Eve, seeing the amber glow in the garden, became frightened.

"It is God, looking for us," Adam said.

"Let us hide," Eve said, and they hid behind a tree.

Serpent remained where he was. He had nothing to worry about. No one had told him not to eat the fruit.

"Adam? Eve?" the Shekina said. "Why are you hiding?"

She knew the answer. She asked just to open a conversation with them, to learn what was in their hearts. Were they sorry they had disobeyed God? Did they regret their act? If they were, she would lessen their punishment.

They had no words of regret. "We are ashamed of our nakedness," they replied.

"Shame? Shame? Where did this feeling come from?" the Shekina said. "I did not make you with shame. You must have done something wrong. Did you eat the fruit I told you not to eat?"

Each blamed the other.

"Eve gave it to me," Adam said.

"Serpent told me to eat it," Eve said.

"I didn't force you," Serpent said.

"Serpent told me it was the tree of knowledge," Eve said. "Since he ate the fruit, I thought he knew everything."

"Only I know everything," the Shekina said.

Serpent, feeling uneasy, looked up at the sky.

Adam said to the Shekina, "Will we die for eating the—"

"The fruit is innocent, do not name it," she said. "I do not want future generations to say, '"Because of this fruit the world suffers."'

The term "future generations" caught Eve's attention. "Where will the future generations come from?" she said. "Adam and I are the only humans, and we are about to die."

"I am letting you live because you have not had time to learn right and wrong," the Shekina said.

Adam and Eve felt a surge of love for God.

"We promise never again to eat the fruit," Eve said.

"Or name it or touch it," Adam said.

"Your promise is wasted," the Shekina said. "You will not be here to keep it. I am banishing you from the garden—where you ate from the fruit-giving trees, walked in pleasant lanes, and breathed fragrant air—and putting you outside, amid thorns and thistles, rot and decay, and where you will have to work hard to get food."

Serpent trembled. The space before him that had contained Adam and Eve was empty.

"Well," he said, "they deserved it."

"And you deserve no mercy," the Shekina said. "You know right from wrong, and you set out to do wrong. You mocked me and told lies."

Serpent tried to speak, but rattling noises came from his throat. His legs disappeared, his body fell to the ground, and he became a long scaly thing. He who had been the cleverest creature in the garden, the only creature who could walk and talk with humans, crawled away on his belly, hissing and eating dust.

In heaven, the Holy One said to the angels, "My plan shapes itself. The humans now know that shame hurts. Perhaps shame will keep them from choosing evil."

CHAPTER 6
The Archangel Brings Seeds to Adam and Eve

Standing outside the garden, Adam and Eve knew only that God was their maker. They knew nothing more and had no memory of a former time. They felt an emptiness, a longing, but did not know for what. They felt hunger but did not know how to get food. As they stood gazing about at the rocky ground and thorny plants, goats came and began nibbling on the plants.

"They are eating it," Eve said.

"I will get us some," Adam said. He thrust his hand into the thorns and pulled it out with a cry. "It is food for animals, not for humans," he said, licking his torn flesh.

The Holy One felt sorry for them.

"Michael," he said to the archangel. "Go down and bring them seeds from the garden. Feed them, and teach them."

With four flaps of her wings Michael was in the garden. She came before Adam and Eve and said, "I am angel Michael, messenger of God. He sends you this gift of food."

She tossed seeds on the ground, and up sprang a field full of cucumbers. "Eat and satisfy your hunger, then I will teach you how to get food," she said.

Michael gave Adam and Eve seeds.

Adam and Eve ate, and when they were through Michael gave them seeds and said, "Remove the rocks, clean the ground, and put these inside. No cucumber field will spring up, as this did, but food will grow in its time." Then she led Adam and Eve around, showing them where to plant, saying, "This is good for a sycamore tree. Here, carob will grow nicely. Here, wheat and barley will grow."

Missing heaven, yearning to return to Glory, to closeness to the Holy One, she left abruptly.

With the flap of her wings sounding in their ears, Adam and Eve set to work, cleaning and planting. They learned from the beasts and from the fowl of the air. Seeing a bird make a nest for itself, they collected grasses and made the walls of a hut. Seeing the outstretched wings of an eagle throw shade on the ground, they laid branches across the walls and were sheltered from the sun.

Wild animals wandered over, and they had sheep and goats and dogs. They had two sons, Cain and Abel.

Satan paid frequent visits. Which boy, Cain or Abel, would serve his purpose? Whose evil urge could he arouse more easily? Not the boy Abel. He was too timid, sitting quietly and stroking his dog. Cain was the one, always in motion, running with his dog, throwing sticks for it to catch.

Satan stirred up in Cain a dislike for his brother, filling his ear with whisperings. "Your parents like Abel better. Abel is their favorite." When the boys were older and Abel had become a shepherd and Cain a worker in the fields, Satan changed his whisperings. Mornings, when Abel took his dog and left with the sheep, Satan whispered to Cain, "See him going to wander with his sheep and gaze at the sky. And you? Toiling in the fields, planting barley, cutting wheat, laying out figs to dry."

The whisperings set Cain's teeth on edge. At the end of the day, when the brothers returned from their work, Cain mocked Abel and called him names. Abel did his best to ignore Cain, but sometimes the insults hurt him and he shouted back.

The arguing was hard for Adam and Eve to bear. Adam built a separate hut for each boy to keep them apart. The brothers came together only for the evening meal, and at the time of the new moon—the time to offer up sacrifices to God.

One day, when a new moon was expected in the sky, Abel returned home early to sacrifice. The sight of embers burning on the family altar told him his mother and father had already sacrificed. The absence of a dog leaping and barking in front of Cain's door told him his brother was not yet home.

Abel chose a healthy young lamb from his flock and offered it up to God. Sacrificing gave him a feeling of peace. He sat down outside his hut to enjoy it. Also pleasing was the sight of his dog at his feet, the aroma of roasting meat in the air, and the songs of birds.

Cain's dog, leaping and barking, broke his reverie. The arrival of Cain wiped it out altogether. Sniffing as he passed the altar, Cain said to Abel, "You have wasted another good lamb."

Abel said nothing. With Cain, that was best. The flock was his, he tended it, and he could do as he pleased.

Cain went into his hut and slept for a while. When he woke, he heated grains in a pot and ate. And what he did not eat, what was left in the pot, he took outside and sacrificed to God.

Abel, watching, could not remain silent. "Leftovers?" he said, offended. "Is this a fit sacrifice for God?"

"God doesn't care," Cain said. "You are a fool, sacrificing a good lamb."

"Nothing is too good for God," Abel said.

"A bird can swoop down and snatch your sacrifice away," Cain said.

"I keep watch—" Abel said.

"Keeping watch, that is all you are good for," Cain said. "Fool!" he shouted, and ran off laughing. Angry, Abel got up and ran after him. The dogs, taking it for a game, ran with them.

Satan had cleared the path for Abel so that Abel ran well, gaining on Cain. And when he was close, Satan whispered to Cain, "Will you let the shepherd overtake the man of the field?"

Cain, turning, saw Abel behind him. He picked up a stone and threw it at his brother's head. Abel fell to the ground.

His work over for the time being, Satan left.

"Get up!" Cain said to his brother as Abel's dog circled his master, whimpering, nuzzling him.

"Get up!" Cain repeated to his brother, annoyed. He did not know Abel was dead. He had seen dead animals, but never a dead human. No human had ever died before. When all his yelling and kicking failed to rouse Abel, it came to him that his brother was dead. The thought frightened him. What would his parents say? Afraid to find out, he took his dog and began to run with him.

But he did not get far.

The eyes of heaven had witnessed the world's first murder. Another disappointment for the Holy One. The Shekina went down to find out what was in the murderer's heart. Did he regret his act? Did he feel remorse?

"You can run from your parents, but not from me," the Shekina said to Cain.

Frightened, Cain fell to his knees.

"Where is your brother?" asked the Shekina.

Foolish Cain, thinking he could deceive God, said, "I do not know. Am I my brother's keeper?"

"You have taken your brother's life and must pay for it with your own," the Shekina said.

"Why didn't you stop me?" Cain said. "You know all. You see everything."

"You could have stopped yourself," the Shekina said.

"But I didn't know Abel would die," Cain said. "When I throw stones at animals, they don't die. They run away."

The Shekina considered his words. What he said was so. He did not know that humans could die. "Because you did not know, I will spare your life," she said.

"What shall I tell my mother and father?" Cain said.

"Tell them?" the Shekina said. "You will never see them again. You have done evil and must be punished."

"What will you do to me?" Cain said, crying.

"You have done it to yourself," the Shekina said. "From this moment on you will live alone and lonely, like a beast, wandering from place to place. Go, and never let me see your face again."

Cain wept fresh tears. "You are everywhere," he said. "Where can I go that you are not?"

The Shekina was silent.

Cain rose. "Why have you saved me?" he said. "So wild beasts may devour me?"

The Shekina marked his forehead with an S and said, "When they see this, they will not touch you."

Cain took his dog and walked off in the direction of Nod.

Now, it was growing dark, and Adam and Eve began to wonder why they had not seen their sons all evening. They went out to look for them and saw Abel's dog in the distance and hurried there. When they saw that Abel's dog was standing guard over Abel's lifeless body—and that the earth was wet with blood—they fell to the ground sobbing.

When they could weep no more, they rose to go but did not feel right about leaving Abel alone. What should they do? Stay with him? Leave him? Go in and take his body with them?

A raven came and scratched a hole in the ground. It flew off, returned with a dead bird between its feet, and buried it in the hole.

Adam and Eve understood what they must do. They took Abel's lifeless body and buried it.

CHAPTER 7
Adam and Eve Also Had Daughters

Now, when Cain was seen to be missing, a sister went in search of him.

A sister?

Just so.

But Adam and Eve had only two sons, Cain and Abel.

Not so. They had daughters as well.

Where is this written?

In the Emerald Book of Secrets.

What is that?

The secret history of heaven and earth. The archangels Michael and Gabriel write the secrets. Record-Keeper Angels write in births, names, and places. Under *Births*, written in their fine hand, this entry appears:

> The two sons of Adam and Eve were Cain and Abel.
> There were also daughters.

In parentheses, one of them added:

(The Holy One loved the world he had made. The marvels and wonders so appealed to him, he made people to enjoy them. As he said when he created humans, "The fowl of the air and the fish of the sea, what were they created for? Of what use is a table full of food, with no guest to enjoy it?" Of course Adam and Eve also had daughters. If they had only boys, how could they carry out God's command to fill the world with people?)

Noticing that the Record Keepers listed the names of the boys, but not of the girls, Raziel told the Holy One of it. And she pointed out to him the likely reason. "The Record Keepers are all males," she said.

The Holy One issued a command to all angel groups, saying, "Let all groups follow my pattern of creation. I made both men and women. Let all groups reflect this model."

The angels reorganized their groups. Raziel kept a watchful eye on the Record Keepers' entries. The names of girls were often given, but not always. It puzzled her why, under the new arrangement, this should be so.

But, getting back to the early times of Adam and Eve, according to the Emerald Book of Secrets the daughter who went in search of Cain found him in Nod. They married, had children, and a second family entered the world. Adam and Eve also had more children. The children grew up and had children of their own. More families entered the world, and more, and still more. As God had commanded, the world began to fill with people.

But people of what quality? Their behavior did not show that they were made in God's image or that they had features in common with angels. Their behavior was common, selfish, and cruel.

The angels, watching, said nothing.

The Arguers, however, could not keep their thoughts to themselves. "You see, Holy One, we were right," they said. "Not only are they wicked. But for the patch of ground that feeds them, they do not take care of the earth. It was a mistake to make them."

The Holy One, ever kind, ever gracious, made excuses for the humans. "They are like a young fig tree," he said, "which puts out thorns before it gives fruit."

The Holy One watched the earth and watched it and among the many found only one good person, Enoch, son of Cain. The others were selfish and cruel.

"These thorns will not become fruit," the Holy One said to the angels. "But Enoch finds favor in my eyes. Him I will remove from the pit of evil and bring him up here, to be with me."

The rays of the amber glow shimmered as the Shekina separated herself from the whole of Glory, went down to earth, and returned with Enoch in her arms.

The Arguers, unfamiliar with the plan, became indignant when they sensed the arrival of an alien presence. Sniffing, they said, "Heaven is for angels. What is this smell of human flesh?"

In a rare display of impatience, the Holy One said, "You have been quarrelsome from the beginning."

The Arguers blushed with shame. They had no say in the workings of heaven. Would they never learn to hold their tongues?

The Holy One relieved their embarrassment. "The humans I have made have turned against me," he said, explaining. "They do not love goodness, but rush to do evil. Only he, only Enoch, is good. I took him as a reward for my labors."

The Arguers could not speak for the wave of love that washed over them.

"Enoch," the Holy One said. "I rename you Metatron and make you a prince in heaven. Your duty will be to watch the earth and decide which humans to reward with greatness, royalty, rank, glory, honor, and praise."

"Oh, Great One, I do not refuse, I dare not refuse," Metatron said. "But I beg you, do not ask this of me."

"Why do you say this?" the Holy One asked.

"If I had such power, people would begin worshiping me instead of you," Metatron said.

From the twinkling and sparkling at the Holy Curtain, the angels knew that Metatron's answer had pleased the Holy One.

"Then I will put you in charge of the Emerald Book of Secrets," the Holy One said.

Heaven vibrated with affection. Whatever pleased the Holy One pleased the angels. Except for the handful of misfits, there was no jealousy among them, no clinging to tasks. Michael, Gabriel, and the Record Keepers were glad to give up the Emerald Book of Secrets. But they did not turn it over directly to Metatron. They let Raziel, who loved ceremonies, do it.

"You give it to him," they said to her.

Raziel held up the glittering face of the Emerald Book of Secrets for all to see. Then, with great solemnity, she handed it to Metatron and called to the Heavenly Chorus, "Singers! Musicians! Let us welcome the prince with a song."

Heaven filled with sweet sound as the musicians made harp and bell-like sounds with their lips and the choir sang six times, "Hail, Metatron, prince of heaven. Hail, heavenly prince."

All angels joined in for the seventh chorus, with the Arguer Angels singing louder than the rest.

CHAPTER 8
Lying—God Did Not Create That

Heaven watched the earth fill with people. The sight did not please the Holy One.

"They are quick to do evil, but to do good, they never heard of it," he said.

"Their faces are sour with hatred and jealousy," the angels said. "And the fighting! The fighting!"

"And see there, where the judge sits," Raziel said. "The man swears that he has seen a thing when he has not seen it."

"And there, the merchant," said archangel Gabriel, "telling the customer the ring is gold when he knows it is copper."

"And what of the customer?" said archangel Uriel. "She pays him with two sheep, swearing they are healthy, when she knows they are diseased and will soon die."

"And the false stories they tell about their neighbors," Rafael said. "What is it, Holy One, this false telling?"

"It is lying," the Holy One replied.

"But you did not make them with lying," said archangel Michael. "Where did they get it?"

The angels knew how Satan occupied himself on earth. "Did Satan teach it to them, Holy One?" asked Michael.

"They taught it to themselves," the Holy One said.

Below, as evening came to earth, the people prepared for worship.

"See how they lie and cheat all day, then go to sacrifice," the Holy One said. "Children gather firewood, fathers kindle fires, mothers bring out cakes to sacrifice to the gods. And who are their gods?"

The angels could not bear the subject.

"A tree that I created," the Holy One said. "A clay figure they have made with their own hands. And if the god they worship does not give them what they want, what do they do?"

No angel spoke. No angel had to. All heaven knew the shameful answer. There was a god called Moloch, an idol with outstretched arms. His belly was a fireplace. They sacrificed their children to Moloch.

The angels could have cried for the Holy One. How the practice offended him! Even the Arguer Angels, who liked to point out that they had been against the idea of creating humans, were silent. The Holy One was hurting enough.

Raziel wanted so to lift the Holy One's spirits. "Wouldn't an entertainment be in order?" she said to the angels. They were quick to respond. The singers and musicians filled heaven with sweet song. Flame Angels danced across the heavens and from heaven to heaven. Wheel Angels rolled about, creating dazzling patterns. Raziel told amusing stories. The Arguer Angels, to produce sounds of enjoyment, laughed louder than was called for.

The Holy One was moved by their love. But all their love could not change the behavior of the humans.

"Only a flood will wipe out the wickedness," he said to the angels. "I will send a flood to drown them all."

Prince Metatron, keeper of the Emerald Book of Secrets, entered the decision in the book. He added a comment of his own:

The decision to send a flood grieves the Holy One. He will look for reasons to delay, even to cancel it. That is his way. But the decision is a just one. I have seen with my own eyes the wickedness of the people. They deserve to drown. Let no one say that the Holy One is cruel. For he is good and kind. He is patient, loving, and merciful.

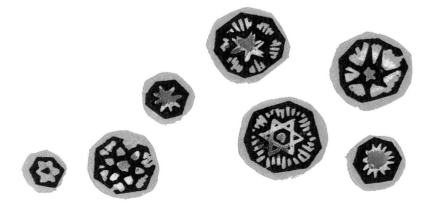

CHAPTER 9
Good King Methuselah

Pained by the decision to send a flood, the Holy One searched the earth for some reason to soften his decision, to delay it, even to cancel it. Again and again, he sent his gaze over the land. And one day, he found what he had been looking for.

"Here is a family that is better than the rest," he said.

Excited, the angels flew to the edges of heaven to see for themselves. They found a family working together, side by side, in an apple orchard. It was Noah and Naamah, their three sons, and the sons' wives.

"They are good, caring people," the Holy One said.

The angels, accustomed to seeing people use their hands to turn the earth, saw this family work differently.

"They use an object to work the soil," they said.

The Holy One knows all, and knew how the object had come into being.

"It is a tool that Noah invented," he said. "It makes the work of planting easier."

The angels knew how this pleased the Holy One. A useful invention puts goodness into the world. Watching the family, the angels saw affection pass between them. They saw one hasten to take up the task another could not finish. And, won-

der of wonders, when their work was over, they did not rush home to feed themselves. They fed the animals first.

"Holy One," Raziel said. "What has made these people good, when the others are so wicked?"

"Their teacher and their own hearts," the Holy One said.

"Their teacher? Who is that?" the angels asked.

"Noah's grandfather, King Methuselah. See him there, sitting with the children of his land."

The angels looked and saw King Methuselah, surrounded by children, teaching them songs of goodness that he had composed. The children repeated after him:

> If you hear people speak bad words
> do not listen, walk away,
> let the wind hear what they have to say.
>
> Whose fingers will steal,
> their lips will lie.
>
> Give one, get two.
> What is it?
> An act of kindness.

In the king's presence, the children remained sweet and kind and affectionate. But when they returned home and saw shouting, hitting, and hateful glances, they shouted, hit, and sent out hateful glances.

"Holy One," Gabriel said. "Since you have found one good family, will you cancel the flood?"

"No, but I will delay it, for Methuselah's sake," the Holy One said. "He will live for another one hundred and twenty years. I will send the flood when he dies. Then I will save the family and start a new world with them."

Every angel heart swelled with love for the Holy One. They understood what he had done. The decision served two purposes: he blessed Methuselah, and also gave people plenty of time to change and give up their wicked ways.

"Metatron," the Holy One said. "Make a copy of the Emerald Book of Secrets for the family. In their copy, leave out the innermost secrets of heaven."

Raziel had never left the Great Heaven. She had no wish to remove herself from Glory, even for an instant. But, as she watched Metatron write, she felt a desire to take the book down to the family. At the same time, the thought of parting with the Holy One distressed her. Then she reminded herself: time does not exist in heaven. If she went down and came back, it would be as if she had never been away.

"Besides," she told herself, "the Holy One knows that I love him. And that my chief joy, my only joy, my sweetest joy is to be near him."

When Metatron finished writing, she made her request. "Holy One," she said. "The family that has pleased you—they have become dear to me. May I take the book down to them?"

"Do so," the Holy One said. "And remain with them while they read the instructions. They will have questions."

Raziel tucked the Emerald Book of Secrets under one wing, gave a flap with the others, and flew down.

CHAPTER 10
The Emerald Book of Secrets, What Was It?

With the Emerald Book under her wing, Raziel appeared before the good family and said, "I am angel Raziel, messenger of God. God is sending a flood to drown the wicked world. But he will save your good family and start a new world with you."

"We are grateful," Noah said, speaking for all. "But a flood is everywhere. How will he drown others, and save us?"

"You will save yourselves," Raziel said. "Build an ark."

An ark? The family had many questions. An ark to do what? How big? How wide? Of what material?

Raziel produced the Emerald Book from under her wing and gave it to Noah.

"It glitters," he said, turning the book over in his hands. "It is beautiful, but what is it?"

"It contains all the secrets of the past and future world," she said. "Read aloud the instructions for building the ark."

The family gathered around Noah as he opened the book and began to read: "Make the ark of cedar wood. Cover it inside and out with pitch. Make it three stories high. Slant the roof, so the rainwater will run down. Let the family occupy the top story. Make a window there and also closets to store food. The middle story is for the creatures, the bottom, for refuse."

Noah looked up. "Creatures?" he said.

"Read on," said Raziel.

"Let me," Naamah said, taking the book and continuing: "Bring along every living creature, at least two of each kind, male and female." She paused and looked up.

"Every creature?" she asked.

"Every single one," Raziel said.

Men and women alike shuddered.

"Creepers and crawlers too?" asked a wife.

"Also," the angel said.

"But surely not the evil creatures?" said Naamah.

"Or the spirits and evil winds?" said a son.

"Not the demons?" said his wife.

"All means all," said Raziel. "Including the punishments, Ashmodai, king of the demons, his wife, Lilith, and all their helpers. Including also the Eyeless Dragon, the Fiery Beasts, the Unima, the Wild Rooster."

The family had never heard these names before.

"Unima? Wild Rooster?" Noah said.

Naamah glanced down at the list of creatures that God had created. "Those are not named here," she said.

"Not all creatures are listed in your copy," Raziel said. "Besides, not all demons are punishments. Some are benefits."

The family knew only evil demons. "How can demons be benefits?" a son asked.

"Unima is a furry creature with the head of a serpent, two tails, and human hands and feet," Raziel said. "She braids and unbraids her tails but cannot turn her head to see behind herself. So she runs around herself all day, trying to catch sight of her tails."

The family exchanged puzzled glances.

"Where is the benefit in that?" Noah asked.

"Humans are not God's only creation," Raziel said. "He made trees as well. Unima's spinning creates a breeze. The trees love the moving air. It refreshes them, and they dance for joy."

"And the Wild Rooster?" Naamah said.

"Ah, that is a human benefit," Raziel said. "The Wild Rooster has in his keeping the Shamir, a worm that splits stone. When Wild Rooster sees a mountain where nothing grows, where there is nothing for people to enjoy, he puts down the Shamir. The worm wriggles across the surface, cracking it. In some cracks, plants and flowers grow. In others, bees leave honey."

"Punishments or benefits," Naamah said. "Demons are invisible. How will we round them up to take them?"

"Do not concern yourselves about that," Raziel said. "Our forces will round them up and install them. Just build a separate room for them on the middle floor. When you see the door of the room close, write on it, *Senoi, Sansenoi, Semaangelof.* The words will seal them in until after the flood."

Noah's thoughts were on the work that lay ahead in building the ark. The Shamir would come in handy. "We will need to chop down cedars and cut planks of wood," he said. "Will Wild Rooster lend us the Shamir to help?"

"You will need no help," Raziel said. "God will not send the flood while King

Methuselah lives. And there yet remain to him one hundred and twenty years, time enough for you to build the ark yourselves." She flapped her wings to fly off, then paused.

"God did not authorize me to say this," she said. "It grieves his heart to send a flood. But people will see you building the ark and ask what it is for. He hopes, when you tell them, that they will repent and ask to be taken along."

She flew off, her sweet angel voice calling after her, "Guard the book carefully."

The family set to work. There was much chopping and cutting to do. Noah had created an ax to make the work easier. They made buckets to hang outside the window to catch the rain, so they would have water for drinking and washing. Chopping and cutting and fitting, they put down three floors, built stalls on the middle floor, plus a room for the demons. On the top floor, they constructed rooms for themselves with a window. They covered the shell of the ark with wood. They cooked and baked and dried food to take along on the journey.

The sons collected seeds and fig and olive saplings for planting after the flood.

"Bring also vine branches," Noah called after them.

After gathering plants, Naamah and the daughters-in-law returned with herbs and cinnamon to add taste to their food and with the bark of sweet-smelling trees to make the air on the ark fragrant.

The finished ark stood three stories high. The assembled animals, several of some kinds, stood in the yard outside the ark. Food for humans and animals had been stored in the storerooms—straw for camels, vine tendrils for elephants, barley for donkeys, shrubs for gazelles, sand for ostriches, and other suitable foods.

The animals were now quiet, but there had been problems at first. They had refused to be confined in the yard. They wanted to roam free. The only animal who didn't complain was the one who changed them. Donkey, by her behavior, taught them patience. Speaking softly, she told them they should feel honored to have been chosen for the journey. She told them that being confined now would help them adjust to the small space on the ark later. Her words persuaded the animals to make plans of their own, to help.

When Methuselah died, the angels wept, their tears falling to earth as a light rain. The family mourned for seven days, then laid down the ramp to the ark. The rain grew heavier as the animals carried one another in, small creatures riding the backs of larger ones. The family led them to their stalls on the middle floor. From a distance, the family watched the door of the demons' room. When they saw it close, they wrote on the door the words the angel had told them to write, *Senoi, Sansenoi, Semaangelof.*

Everyone was inside the ark, except for Noah, who was standing downstairs in the doorway. Naamah and the women were seated around the table on the third floor. The animals were in their places on the middle floor. The sons went down to take up the ramp.

"Not yet," Noah said to them, peering into the heavy rain. "Someone may yet come, asking to be taken along."

"Father," said a son. "They have all seen the ark."

"They all know what it is for," said another son.

"They did not ask then, and do not ask now, when they can see large pools of water on the ground," said the third.

The rain was now falling so hard, the ark began to lift. The sons took up the ramp. Noah closed the door, and father and sons went up to the third floor to join the family.

CHAPTER 11
Satan Accompanies the Ark

The rains fell and the waters rose and rose, covering the face of the earth. The ark floated along peacefully on top of the waters.

Unknown to the passengers inside the ark, they had invisible company outside the ark.

Satan and his followers had nothing to fear from the flood. Angels, even fallen angels, live forever. They cannot drown. What they did fear was boredom, having nothing to do, having no one to work their mischief on, being unable to cause trouble. They needed people for that. The only people left in the world were on the ark. So when the ark came floating by Mount Hermon, the followers turned themselves into bubbles and bounced along beside it. Satan rode the foam.

There were others. The great creatures were also present. Swimming along outside the ark with the dolphins and whales and sea animals large and small was the great fish, Leviathan. Behemoth, the great land creature, lay stretched out on the roof of the ark, resembling a vast cloud. And Ziv of the great wingspan flew unnoticed in the meadows of the sky.

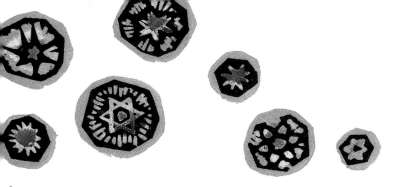

CHAPTER 12
The Animals Have to Be Fed

The family was kept so busy on the ark, they had little time to rest. The day was taken up with washing, cleaning, and tidying up. Feeding the animals took the most time. The first few times they went down to feed the animals, they went all together as a group. They were afraid to pass the demons' room. But as they crept by the door marked *Senoi, Sansenoi, Semaangelof* they heard nothing on the other side. No sound or movement of any kind. The silence made them bold, and they became courageous enough to go down in small groups.

The sons fed the night animals. The wives fed the others. Keeping peace between the creatures, the most difficult task, fell to Noah and Naamah.

One day, the mouse came crying to Naamah. The cat had struck her with a paw and ripped her cheek. "Bring me a hair from the tail of the swine," Naamah said. When the mouse returned with the hair, Naamah sewed up the tear with it. That is how the mouse came by the seam at the side of her mouth.

Another time, Noah noticed a phoenix slumped over in a dark corner looking hungry.

"Do my children not feed you?" he said.

"It is not their fault," the phoenix said. "They have so much to do, they don't notice me. I cannot bring myself to add to their many duties."

Moved by the tender words, Noah blessed the phoenix. "May the almighty Creator grant you eternal life for your goodness," he said.

To this day, the phoenix does not die. It goes up in flames but rises immediately from its own ashes and lives again.

Accidents on the ark changed the features of some animals permanently. The moles lost their eyes forever, and frogs their teeth. The raven's accident was his own fault. He was jealous of the graceful walk of the dove and tried to imitate him. He fell over and injured himself. Noah treated his injuries. When he could walk again, he could only hop. And that is how ravens walk to this day.

When the family finished the day's work, they went up to their floor, the third floor with the window. While it was still light, they ate and watched the falling rain. When night came, they opened the Emerald Book of Secrets. Its glitter lit up even the darkest corner. By its light, they read the secrets of the world and details about the flood: what course it would take, how long it would last, and what they should expect.

The rain stopped falling on the fortieth day, as the Emerald Book had said it would. When the ark came to an abrupt halt, they knew they had landed on Mount Ararat. Day by day they watched from the window to see the waters go down and down, until one day, at last, they saw the dear face of the earth again.

"We must wait for the earth to dry," Noah said, reminding them that the earth would be mud for four days.

As restless as they had been to leave the ark, when the four days were over, no one wanted to be first to go down.

"How can we be sure it's dry?" they said.

"It might look dry, but we could be swallowed up in the mud," they said.

"Let us wait another two days."

"Another four days might be wiser."

"Enough," Noah said. "We will send out a dove."

"What good will that do?" Naamah said. "Birds live in trees, we live on the ground."

"The dove likes the ground," Noah said. "When she returns, we will see if her feet are muddy or dry."

He caught a white dove that was flying by and sent her out through the window. She returned with an olive branch in her beak and dry feet. (And where did she get the olive branch? She had flown to Jerusalem and plucked the branch from a tree on the Mount of Olives.)

"The dryness of her feet tells us that we may leave," Noah said. He opened the door of the ark. "Let the animals out first."

The sons put down the ramp, and the animals went out two by two and spread out over the face of the earth, finding new lairs and dens and coves and habitats for themselves. The great creatures returned to their places, Leviathan to monitor the deep, Behemoth to patrol the earth, and Ziv passing unnoticed in the clouds.

The family went up and down, removing their belongings. As they passed the middle floor, they saw the demons' door slide open and the words *Senoi, Sansenoi, Semaangelof* disappear from it. Naamah brought out the food that remained and the seeds and saplings for planting. Noah went down with the vine branch for planting in one hand and the Emerald Book of Secrets in the other.

Standing on the ground, the family was silent, looking about one another.

The dove returned with an olive branch and dry feet.

Words did not seem to be enough to express their feelings. They could only hug one another and themselves and stomp on the ground, making contact with the earth underfoot.

"We must sacrifice to God, to thank him," Noah said.

The family began gathering stones for an altar. They all paused and looked at one another. The same thought had occurred to all of them: they would have to slaughter an animal for the sacrifice. How could they do that? The animals had become their friends. They knew the names of each one.

The animals saw their dilemma and took matters into their own hands. They were also God's creation. They also had a wish to serve God.

"I have lived long enough," said a sheep. "Sacrifice me."

"Sacrifice me, too," said another.

"Take me," said a pigeon.

"If you take her, take me," said her mate.

The matter was resolved.

The family proceeded to build an altar, chanting, as they set down stone after stone:

> These two thank God for saving the world.
> These two thank God for saving the creatures.
> These two thank God for saving our family.
> These two thank God for setting our feet down on the earth.
> These two thank God for the wonderful world he has made.

And the place where they built the altar—where was it? In the same place where the altar of Adam and Eve had stood. Where Cain and Abel had sacrificed.

The aroma of roasting meat filled the air, and God saw smoke rising up from the altar, the family's sign of gratitude.

He spoke to them. "The people were wicked and deserved to drown," he said. "But the earth was innocent. It had done no wrong, and should not have drowned with them. Such a thing will never happen again."

And he placed a bow in the sky. "This shall be a sign of my promise, to all future generations," he said.

The family was in raptures over the bow, an ark of raindrops that the sun filled with soft colors.

Noah spoke for the family. "For ourselves and our descendants, we make this promise in return: We will worship only you. We will teach justice and kindness. We will let honest judges settle our disputes. We will not kill, commit adultery, steal, or eat flesh cut from living animals."

God looked at the family. He had faith in them. Perhaps their descendants would be good, kind, and caring, the sort of people he could love. For the second time in human history, God said, "Have children, and fill my world with people."

Noah and Naamah, the sons and their wives, all built homes near one another. They worked the earth and planted. Orchards and groves and vineyards began to appear. The sons and their wives had children, their children had children, and the world once more hummed with life and movement.

CHAPTER 13
Satan's Followers Team Up with Demons

After the flood, Satan noticed his followers teaming up with the demons. He was glad to be rid of them. They were always bothering him, always wanting to come along on his projects. He did not need them. They were only in the way.

"Good riddance," he thought, listening to them exchange secrets with their partners.

"Tricks and temptations," the demons taught his followers.

"Color a stone like a jewel and dangle it over a pit."

"Polish brass to make it gleam like gold."

"Cause a mirage, and when they come near, yank it away."

The followers taught the demons cures:

"To protect against fire, smear the skin with the blood of a salamander."

"If the one-eyed yellow beast attacks, throw ashes in its face."

"What the crawling snail secretes, that cures boils."

"For a hornet sting, crush a fly to powder, and apply it."

Satan laughed. "Boils and ashes," he said to himself. "They have no imagination. I have caused the downfall of the first world population and will do so again with this one. Only I'll do it more quickly this time."

He meant by this that no longer would he go sniffing around a person searching for a weakness that would allow him to arouse the evil urge of the individual. That took too long and was too troublesome. He had found a better way. He would attach himself to a leader and arouse the leader's evil urge. The rest took take care of itself. Whatever people saw their leaders do, they also did.

Satan attached himself to Noah and Naamah and filled their ears with whisperings. "You are special," he said. "You have been chosen. On account of your goodness, the world has been saved."

As he intended, Noah and Naamah became conceited and haughty. They began to speak endlessly about themselves, annoying their sons, their daughters-in-law, their grandchildren. After a time, Satan changed his whisperings.

"Your sons and their wives, do they honor you?" he said to Noah. "If they do, why do they let you work, when you are old? They are strong. They have many children to help them. They should work for you and give you an equal share."

Finding these questions in his mind, Noah said to his sons, "Naamah and I are old. Why must we work in the field? Why don't you provide us with food?"

The sons did not have to be persuaded. They were glad to do it. Thereafter, each time there was a new crop—wheat, barley, cucumbers, pomegranates—they filled two baskets and brought them to Noah and Naamah.

When that question was settled in his mind, Noah found new thoughts to trouble him: Were his sons working hard enough? What he and Naamah were receiving, was it an even share—or less than what the sons were taking for themselves? He began appearing at the field to watch his sons work. Whatever they did, he found fault with it, saying he could do it faster and better. The sons began to dread Noah's visits.

Naamah had received other whisperings and found other questions in her mind. It seemed to her that her daughters-in-law were talking about her and making fun of her. She began to go each morning to the house of one daughter-in-law or another and spend the day there, throwing out questions to test the women, looking for hidden movements, studying the faces of the children for secret meanings. The daughters-in-law and their children dreaded Naamah's visits.

Noah and Naamah spoke openly about their suspicions. With proddings from Satan, they soon began to doubt each other. They spoke in half sentences if they had something to say. They did not look at each other when they spoke. Soon, they stopped speaking altogether.

Noah became concerned about the Emerald Book of Secrets that the angel had left with him. She had entrusted it to his care, but into whose hands would it fall when he was gone? No one was worthy of it. No one deserved the honor. The grandchildren were as mean and grasping as their parents. One morning, he waited for Naamah to leave the house. When she was gone, and everyone was working in the field or busy at their labors, he took the book outside and buried it.

No one asked about the book. No one missed it. They were all too busy spying on one another, spreading stories, quarreling.

Satan had done his work well. The good family that God had saved from the flood was no longer good. Not they, not their children, not their grandchildren. They had broken every promise Noah had made to God, except one. And that they kept not out of love but out of habit. They still sacrificed to God.

On the coming of the new moon, Satan again went to work.

Each family sacrificed to God on its own altar. By means of the sacrifice, they asked God for help. Satan turned himself into a breeze and went from altar to altar dropping the same words into each ear: "What is this? You sacrifice to God. They sacrifice to God. It is not good. If God favors them, how can he favor you? Make a god for yourself who will be your god, who will take care of you."

It was not long before they began making gods for themselves. The main gods were Baal, his round-bellied wife, Asherah, and Baal's father, the bull god. The relatives and children of these were also gods. To make their gods important in the eyes of others, the men made feasts and ceremonies on the new moon. Women put on perfume and sang to the gods. They put bells on their ankles and did wild dances to please them.

The singing and the sounds of merriment attracted Satan's followers. When they smelled the perfume and saw the dancing they fell in love with the women. At once, they turned themselves into men and married the dancers. The one thing they could not change in themselves was their calves' feet, a permanent feature of angels, even of former angels. But their feet were kept hidden, for their wives had taught them to wear shoes, how to eat, and other wordly ways. The former angels taught their wives how to cast spells and raise boils on human flesh. Their children were born restless and with mouths full of hatred. They married each other and invented evils never dreamed of before.

Satan's followers turned themselves into men.

CHAPTER 14
Noah's Vine Branch

The cool weather set in. Grapes, Noah's favorite fruit, were ready for picking. When Noah saw his sons go to the vineyard with baskets and begin to pick grapes, he went to watch. Only that way could he be sure that his basket and Naamah's received the same amount of grapes as the others.

As Noah stood watching, Satan came and whispered in his ear, "Grapes are good not only for eating. Press them, and let them stand. They become wine. Even one sip gladdens the heart."

The sons brought two baskets to their parents' door, but no grape reached Naamah's lips. For when Noah began to make wine with his grapes, Satan whispered, "Not enough. Take hers too."

Without asking Naamah if he could, Noah added her grapes to his. Naamah watched him. Already sour toward him, she soured even more. Again and again she saw him leave the house with an empty basket and return with a basket full of grapes.

The sons watched Noah's comings and goings with mounting anger. They said to one another, "He is spoiling the grape count with his winemaking."

They meant by this that he had reduced their share. There was now less for them to divide up among themselves. They corrected the unfairness. When night fell, each one stole into the vineyard and helped himself to grapes. Thus the vines stood empty before their time and everyone knew why. The brothers cast hateful glances at one another. They stopped working together. Each began to cultivate his own patch. They set dogs out at night to guard the patch.

One day, the cry, "My wine is ready!" came from Noah.

"His wine!" Naamah said, watching from the doorway.

The sons and their wives and their children were bitter, but curious. Everyone stopped work and went to see.

Noah poured wine into a cup and sipped. A warm sensation filled his chest. "It gladdens the heart," he said, for all to hear.

Satan urged him on. "If a cup of wine will gladden your heart, what will a bowl do?" Satan whispered.

Noah brought the cup into the house and came out with a bowl. He filled the bowl with wine, drank, and let out a whoop of enjoyment.

Satan, considering his work over, withdrew.

Noah drank again and began to sing and dance. He drank another bowlful and tried to climb a tree, but fell down. He tried again, and again he fell. After the third try, he remained on the ground laughing to himself. Then he closed his eyes and went to sleep.

"Carry him inside," Naamah said.

The sons felt such bitterness for their father, they did not want to touch him.

"Pick him up," Naamah said.

They came forward grudgingly, lifted Noah, brought him into the house, and put him on the bed.

Naamah tossed them a blanket and they covered him. Noah laughed and kicked the blanket off himself.

"Leave it," Naamah said harshly, putting the blanket back.

He made a growling noise, kicked off the blanket again, and took off his clothes.

The sons looked away. "You are naked," they said.

"I like it," Noah said.

"Cover yourself," Naamah said, shielding her eyes.

"I will not," Noah said.

Naamah walked away.

The sons left in disgust.

They were not the only ones.

A sigh came from the Holy Curtain that broke the heart of every angel.

"This population is no better than the one I drowned," the Holy One said. Unable to bear the wickedness, he turned away from the world and would not look at it.

CHAPTER 15
A New Class of Angels

The Holy One had turned away from the world, but it was his world—he had made it—and he must know what went on there. For the purpose, he created a new class of angels, Earth Walkers. These angels descended to earth at the start of a new year. Invisible, in groups of three, they spread out over the earth, walking up and down the districts assigned to them, visiting every household. At the end of the year, when the moon was full, they returned to heaven with their reports.

It was now the start of a new year, and the Earth Walkers went down and spread out. The three assigned to Aram found a banquet in process when they arrived. They looked it over and saw that it was a banquet to honor King Nimrod. Nothing new there. Nimrod often gave banquets for himself. The Earth Walkers left the banquet and went on their way.

Now it happens that Satan was a guest at the banquet. He had attached himself to Nimrod when Nimrod was only the head of a band of warriors. With his whisperings, Satan had guided Nimrod's steps, until Nimrod became king.

Satan was disguised as Adonia, queen of Ethiopia, and seated on the king's left.

Throughout the meal, Satan complimented Nimrod on his cleverness and valor. At the end of the meal, as the servants brought out the sweet cakes, Satan leaned over to Nimrod and said, "Nimrod, the gods favor you. Do not waste it. Declare yourself king of the world."

Nimrod turned to Satan with a smile and patted his hand in reply. The gesture said: I dare not even dream it. And while he meant it at the time, he could not sleep that night for thinking. He was king. He could do whatever he wished. Why should he not declare himself king of the world?

And this he did the next morning, sending his heralds out into the streets to proclaim, "Nimrod the Great is king of the world!"

Nimrod gave himself another banquet to celebrate.

Satan was again among the guests, disguised this time as Angias, wise man of Africa. The king drank heartily of the wine put before him and was in a fine mood. When the dancers came leaping out, clicking their finger bells and slapping tambourines, Nimrod drummed on the table, keeping time to the music. Satan leaned over and whispered, "The world is too small for your greatness. Strive to become king of heaven."

Without missing a beat, without turning his head, Nimrod whispered back, "Heaven is not my place."

These were the words he uttered. And he meant them at the time. But as the guests were leaving, he took Satan aside and said, "Angias, wise man of Africa, how does one win heaven?"

"How did you win earth?" said Satan.

"With bows and arrows," said Nimrod.

"The same way," said Satan.

"Where is such a battlefield?"

"Build a tower to heaven."

The next morning, Nimrod went before the people and said, "Let us build a tower to heaven. Whoever wishes to be known as great, come and build it."

The people responded in droves. They came—men, women, and children—and began working. The women baked bricks, the children passed them along to the men, the men laid them down. Satan floated among them egging them on, whispering, "Finish the tower, make a name for yourselves." The people worked day and night. They worked with a fury, pausing only to ask, "Does it touch the sky yet?"

When the answer came back, "Not yet," they became wild.

They beat men who could not keep up. They made children who rested work through the night. If a woman was slow, they kicked her aside and left her to die.

The Earth Walkers of Aram were astonished at the cruelty they saw. Astonished and deeply saddened. They had finished their rounds and were on the way back, with nothing good to report. Now they must add to it this violence, this cruelty! It would pain the Holy One greatly. It grieved them to be the bearers of such reports. They returned to heaven with heavy hearts.

All Earth Walkers returned at the same time, and all in low spirits. They assembled themselves by region and group by group rose to deliver their reports. Raziel sat outside the Holy Curtain and heard everything. The angels came to listen.

They spoke the truth. Angels do not know how to lie. But out of love for the Holy One, out of a desire to spare his feelings, each group softened its words.

In reporting thievery, they never used the word "steal." They said a person had "taken a thing without permission."

In reports of lying, or false swearing, they said the guilty person "danced around the truth."

When it came to reporting idol worship, they could find no soft words. They spit out the words quickly, to rid their mouths of the offense, saying, "They sacrifice to a bull named Baal, and to a tree called Asherah. And they"—how it distressed the angels to say it!—"sacrifice their children to Moloch."

A great sigh came from the Holy Curtain. "Is there more?"

It was the turn of the Earth Walkers of Aram to speak. Their hearts were too heavy even to look for soft words. They described, plainly, the tower Nimrod was building to heaven, said why he was building it, and reported the workers' cruel and violent behavior in their zeal to finish the tower.

Raziel was overcome with anger. "This is the work of Satan," she said.

The Holy One had heard enough.

"Come. Let us go down and mix up their speech and put a stop to this work," he said.

The Shekina separated herself from the whole of Glory and went down with a band of angels. Like a wind, like the sound of rushing waters, she passed through the workers, confusing their minds and mixing up their speech.

The workers put down their tools. They could not continue. Strange words formed in their mouths. When they tried to ask for a brick, they said "hammer." When they tried to say mortar, they said "two." When they tried to ask for water, they said "noon."

Confused and frightened, they descended the tower and went home to collect their belongings. In a great stream the people left the city, crossed the river Sambatyon, and scattered over the face of the earth. With the new words they now found in their mouths, they started up a new language in each place.

As for the tower, it still stands. Time and war and weather have worn away the upper section. But the base is still there. And it is so high that a person standing on the ground and looking up can hardly see the top of it.

CHAPTER 16
The Idol Shop in Ur

A new year had begun and the Earth Walkers again descended to earth for a round of walking.

The three assigned to Aram found nothing changed. Nimrod was still king. The people were as selfish and greedy as before. How the angels wished they could bring back a report that would please the Holy One! They looked hard for signs of goodness, of nearly good, of someone who maybe, maybe, might become good. They found no such person and continued on to the city of Ur.

The people of Ur were a mix of star worshipers and idol worshipers. The idol worshipers were too impatient to wait for the stars to come out at night in order to worship. They turned to idols because they could keep these in their homes or yards and worship at any time.

They bought their idols in the shop of Terah and Emtelai. This was the Earth Walkers' first stop in Ur. Upon entering, they found the usual sight: Terah sat on one stool, his wife, Emtelai, on another, and all around the shop were idols—serpents, bulls, Baals, Astartes, the love goddesses, and all the lesser gods. The couple's son and daughter-in-law, Abraham and Sarah, were not present. But that was not surprising. They worshiped the stars and often went to the desert to pray.

The angels would come back to see Abraham and Sarah at a later time. They were about to move on, when a customer came and asked for a statue of Moloch. The question made the angels stop and listen.

Terah rose. "You dare come here for a Moloch? The child eater?" he said, indignant.

Emtelai, just as offended, said, "We have only helpful gods here."

The angels looked at each other in surprise. They had heard Terah and Emtelai speak about the power of an idol, the cost of an idol, the size. Never had they heard the two differentiate between good and evil before.

Moved by what they had heard, they went on their way.

The angels had supposed correctly. Abraham and Sarah were in the desert. They were there to worship the group of stars around the planet Jupiter, which to them was the most powerful force in the world. In the desert they could feel the power of the stars. The stillness, the dark nights, the twinkle and glitter in the sky showed their greatness.

As they did each morning, Sarah and Abraham rose while it was still dark and went to sit outside the tent to greet the sun. Sitting and eating their bread and olives in silence, they watched the sun enter the dark sky and slowly, slowly, roll across it, lighting up strips of earth as it went. The camel that had brought Abraham and Sarah to the desert sat chewing its cud.

They had done the same thing many times. Sitting in silence, eating, watching the sun march across the sky. Nothing was different today. Yet today, for some reason, Abraham found himself questioning the power of the stars—the stars he revered and worshiped. He spoke of it to Sarah.

In the desert they could feel the power of the stars.

"Each morning we see the sun wipe the stars from the sky," he said. "How powerful can stars be if the sun is able to do that?"

Sarah's heart stirred. The question had the force of an answer. If the sun could do that, it had to be the more powerful of the two. She had a question of her own.

"How powerful can the sun be, if the moon can wipe it away?"

The thoughts excited them. Questions flew from their lips. "Who gave us knowledge? The ear that hears, who made it? The eye that sees, who made that? Who taught the cock to crow at dawn? The stork, the turtle dove, the swallow, the crane—how can they arrive here the same time each year? How do they know when to set out? How do they know the way? Who gave the bird a voice to sing with?"

Every question led them to the same answer: One great unseen power, one great force, one God, made everything.

They had planned to leave the desert in the late afternoon but were too restless to stay on. They loaded the tent and their belongings onto the camel's back and headed for Ur. As they always did, they stopped at the desert camp of King Melchizedek to rest and refresh themselves. But this time they did more. They spoke with fervor about the knowledge that now filled them, knowledge of the one force, the one power, the one God.

CHAPTER 17
The Earth Walkers Have a Surprise

When the Earth Walkers returned to the idol shop, they found Abraham and Sarah present. A friendly family argument seemed to be taking place. The angels listened.

"But, Father," Abraham said, "there is not one god for rain, another for crops, a third for cattle. There is only one God."

The angels were so astonished, they had to hold down their wings to keep them from flapping.

"The desert sun has cooked their brains," Terah said to his wife.

"What has happened to you two?" Emtelai said, looking from Abraham to Sarah. "People worship idols. Others, like yourselves, worship stars. But this idea of one God—where did you get it?"

"Aunt, Uncle," Sarah said. So she called them, for Abraham was also her cousin. She glanced at the clay figures along the walls. "These idols, are they gods?" she said. "Did they form the world? Did they make mountains and valleys? Do they keep the sun and moon from falling?"

"We know, we know," Terah said with impatience. "You have told us. Your one God made everything."

"And where is he, this one God of yours?" Emtelai asked.

"He fills heaven and earth," Abraham said.

"No spot is free of his presence," Sarah added.

"I have never seen him," Emtelai said.

"He is invisible," Abraham said.

"Invisible?" Terah repeated with a laugh. "Oh, you fools in the world."

"He is spirit, Father," Abraham said. "Spirit is invisible."

"Uncle, Aunt," Sarah said, "can you see the air you breathe? You cannot. But you know it's there."

"A god is powerful, mighty," Emtelai said. "We see signs of his power: a palace, horses, chariots, armies—"

"Tax collectors—" Terah said.

"Nimrod is a god," Emtelai finished.

"So he tells you," Sarah said.

"Mother, Father," Abraham said. "Did Nimrod make the heavens? The seas, did he make them? Did he make the gnat?"

"Enough," Terah said. He rose and went to the door. Emtelai and Sarah followed. They went off to rejoice with Abraham's brother and sister-in-law. A new baby boy, Lot, had been born to them. Abraham had agreed to stay behind and care for the shop.

"Sell many idols," Terah called as they left.

The Earth Walkers had more visits to make in Ur. They were not due back in heaven for a few days. But how could they stay and finish their rounds? They could not. After so many saddening reports, they at last had something to tell that would lift the Holy One's spirits. Forgetting in their excitement to hide the sound of their wings, they flapped largely, stirring the air and making a sound like rushing waters, and flew off.

CHAPTER 18
Abraham Converts the Men, Sarah, the Women

Angel Raziel, sitting outside the Holy Curtain, was surprised to see the Earth Walkers of Ur arrive. "You are early," she said. "The others are still making their rounds."

The Earth Walkers, their voices trembling with excitement, said, "What we have to tell will delight your ears."

Every angel in the seventh heaven looked up. What was this? Why were the Earth Walkers back so soon? And why were they trembly and iridescent?

The Earth Walkers bowed before the Holy Curtain. They stood a moment, trying to compose themselves. It was not seemly to jitter before the Holy Curtain. The voices of heaven were voices of pleasantness.

"Oh, Holy One," they said, their voices rising despite their efforts. "What news we have!"

The angels knew something unusual had taken place. Earth Walkers delivered their gloomy reports in leaden voices. These three from Ur spoke from jaunty hearts. Raziel waited to hear more. The other angels drew closer to listen.

The Holy One was also curious. "Speak," he said.

The three, in their excitement, spoke at once, interrupting one another.

"In the city of Ur, a man and his wife—"

"He, handsome as a white horse with a red ribbon—"

"She, more beautiful than a pomegranate blossom—"

The rays of the amber glow shifted slightly, and the Holy One said, "So far I have heard nothing."

The Earth Walkers calmed themselves. For the sake of order, one spoke for all.

"The man is Abraham, his wife is Sarah," the angel said. "No one has taught them about you. Yet, they know you. All by themselves they have stumbled across you in their hearts. They love you and praise you."

Raziel and the angels could have cried for happiness when they saw the amber glow brighten. The Holy One, their hearts' desire, their beloved, was pleased.

The Holy One had for so long refused to look at the world. Now, hearing these words, he turned with interest toward the world, sending his gaze over Aram, over the city of Ur, and focusing on the idol shop. The angels, following his gaze, looked with him and watched Abraham rise from his stool to greet a customer.

"Peace be yours, Abraham," said the customer.

"And yours as well, my friend," Abraham said. "Is your planting over? Your cucumbers, are they in the ground?"

"They are," the farmer said. "I have done my part, but the goddess Asherah is not able to do hers."

"And why is that?" Abraham asked.

"The wind that came last night," the farmer said. "It knocked her down. She lies in pieces, strewn across my field."

"It is a sad story," Abraham said.

It was an odd response and the farmer looked at him. "I did not come for your sympathy, Abraham," he said. "I came for a new goddess."

"To keep the crows away?" Abraham said.

The farmer again looked at him strangely. "To worship, so she will grant me a good crop," he said.

Abraham went to the Asherahs lined up against the wall. "Which of these would you like?"

The farmer pointed. "That one—"

"It was made this morning," Abraham said.

"This morning, last week, I don't care—" the farmer said, losing patience.

"My friend," Abraham said. "You have been growing cucumbers for fifty years. Woe to you, if you think this day-old idol can help you more than your own two hands."

The farmer became red in the face and left, and as he went out, Plonit the widow came in shaking her head.

"What is this world coming to?" she said. "While I was at the public baths, a thief entered my house and stole my god of protection. Give me a new one, Abraham."

"Good Plonit," Abraham said, "if the god couldn't protect itself from thieves, how can it protect you?"

Plonit was silent.

"Your god is made of clay," Abraham said. "It has a mouth but cannot speak, feet that cannot move, eyes that do not see. It is a dead thing. How can it help you?"

"There are gods," Plonit said. "A person must appeal to them, rely on them—"

"There is only one God," Abraham said. "One God who made heaven and earth and everything in between."

The words entered Plonit's heart. She stood looking at him. "Speak to me of your God," she said after a moment.

Abraham told her of his thoughts, the understanding that had come to him. When he was through speaking, the widow Plonit left without an idol. Watching her go, Abraham saw his parents returning up the lane. Sarah, he knew, had gone home to their tent at the edge of the city. Quickly, Abraham took a stick and went about the shop smashing idols. He left one standing, a large Baal, and put the stick in its hand.

When Terah and Emtelai entered, they were speechless. They stood looking at the floor, covered from end to end with broken idol parts—noses, limbs, chests, arms, heads.

"What is this?" Terah said.

Abraham nodded toward the standing Baal. "He did it," he said. "The idols began arguing about who was the most powerful. To show them who he was, he took a stick and smashed them to bits."

His parents glared at him.

"You fool in the world!" Terah said. "Idols can't argue. They can't hold sticks!"

"They can't do anything," Emtelai said.

"Father, Mother," Abraham said. "Do your ears hear what your mouth is saying?"

The silence that filled the room indicated that Terah and Emtelai had heard. Suddenly, they understood what Abraham and Sarah had been been telling them about the one God.

The attention of heaven remained on Ur as Terah and Emtelai closed the idol shop, as the widow Plonit sealed up her home, and as all three went to help Abraham and Sarah in their tent at the edge of the city.

And what was this tent? A place known to travelers as the Tent of the Servants of God. It was a shelter where visitors arriving thirsty and dusty from the road could receive food and water. When the visitors were refreshed and said, "Thank you," a conversation opened up. And Abraham and Sarah began teaching about God.

"Do not thank us, thank God," they said. "The bread and water are his, he made them."

"How do you know this?"

"The garment you wear, who made it?" they said.

"A weaver, of course."

"How do you know this?" they said.

The travelers, understanding their meaning, said nothing.

"Open your eyes and you will see for yourself," they said. "Study the creatures, the fields and streams, the mountains and valleys, the woods and forests. They will help you see God. Ask the birds of the air, they will tell you. The plants of the earth, they will teach you."

The travelers, listening with interest, asked, "How do we thank him?"

"The food on your table comes from his earth. Thank him when you sit down to eat."

"Where is he, to hear us?"

"He is everywhere."

"No god can be everywhere."

"This God, the one God in heaven, can."

It was a hard thought. The travelers set it aside.

"What does he want of us?"

"He wants you to stop worshiping idols and to worship only him."

"The way we serve the idols, by animal sacrifice?"

"That is just a ceremony. He prefers another way."

"Which is?"

"Your actions. You worship him by being good."

"How does that serve him?"

"He wants to be in the world with us."

"If he can do all that you say, why can't he come down?"

"Our good deeds form an invisible ladder to heaven. On it, we rise up to meet him. On it, he comes down to meet us."

So it went, and so it went.

The amber rays of Glory sparkled merrily as the Holy One said to the angels, "These two are making me known on earth."

CHAPTER 19
God Enters the World

The world was full of idol gods. Each god had its followers. Baal had his, the goddess Asherah had hers, the bull god had his. But God, who made heaven and earth, had no followers until Abraham and Sarah began to speak about him.

When God heard them and saw their behavior, he said to Abraham, "Leave this place where you were born, and go to Canaan. Have children, and found a nation for me there."

Abraham would do it. He would do whatever God asked. But he permitted himself one question.

"Canaan belongs to the Canaanites," he said. "Will they accept a new nation on their land?"

"It is not their land, it is mine," God said. "All the earth is mine. I give a land to whom I wish. When I wish, I take it away and give it to another."

A second question had danced into Abraham's mind, but he did not ask it. He and Sarah loaded their possessions onto the backs of camels and donkeys. They assembled their flocks and cattle. And with three hundred followers, relatives, servants, and strangers who had joined them they set out.

In Canaan, they put up their tents at the edge of Hebron, near some terebinth trees. The spring that flowed under the trees assured them of a source of water. The place had another attraction. A nation must bury its dead. A field with an empty burial cave, the Cave of Machpelah, was for sale.

The neighboring tribes became accustomed to the strangers in their midst. They called them "Servants of God" and knew the men had made a mark in their flesh as a sign that they worshiped God. They saw them sitting around a fire at night, listening to Abraham and Sarah speak about God.

When the teaching was over and others began to tell stories, Abraham only half listened. The question he had failed to ask God still danced in his mind. One night, he spoke of it to Sarah. He valued what she had to say. People in the camp called Sarah "Iscah," or Seer. Her heart told her things no eye could see.

"We have founded a nation for God," he said. "Who will hold it together when when we are gone? We are old and have no children."

"God who sets the heavens in motion will make this right, too," Sarah said.

"But we are too old to have children," Abraham said.

"Nothing is too hard for God," Sarah said, and added, "I am too old. But as an old cinnamon tree can produce fruit, so can an old man if he has a young wife. I will give you my young Egyptian maid, Hagar, for a wife. Have a son with her, and I will raise him as my own."

Hagar was happy to become Abraham's second wife. Abraham was head of the tribe. The two women loved each other and continued as before, Sarah assigning duties and Hagar fulfilling them, until Hagar began to carry Abraham's child.

Now Satan had not disappeared, though he had failed to stir up the evil urge in

Abraham and Sarah. He had used every trick he knew to get them to do wrong, but to no avail. He could not budge them. They loved God and would do nothing to offend him.

But when Hagar became pregnant, he had new details to work with. He filled Hagar's ear with whisperings, saying, "Sarah is no longer your mistress. You are her equal. You are more. She cannot have children and you carry Abraham's child. She is Abraham's first wife, but you are first in his affections."

Satan's whisperings turned Hagar's head. She distanced herself from her former mistress. She went about the camp mocking Sarah, calling her names like "Empty Vessel," "Cow without Milk," "Barren Patch." When her child was born, a boy named Ishmael, she broke her promise. Not only did she refuse to let Sarah raise the child, she did not let Sarah come anywhere near the boy. And the boy, as he grew, was rude to Sarah.

Sarah's heart, which had told her things no eye could see, had been silent on the subject of Hagar.

People spoke in hushed tones of Sarah's unhappiness.

"And Abraham lets it happen?"

"He is upright. He is good. But when it comes to Hagar, or the boy, he pretends not to notice."

God saw the strife in Abraham's tents and said to the archangels Michael, Gabriel, and Rafael, "Go down and make it known that Sarah will have a son."

The archangels went down disguised as foot travelers and came upon Abraham sitting outside his tent. As was his way, he leapt up to welcome the three strangers and gave them food to eat and water to drink. Later, when the three men rose to go, they took angel dust from themselves and marked the tent with it.

"Next year, when the rays of the sun touch this mark, Sarah will give birth to a son," they said.

Sarah, standing in the door of her tent, heard them and laughed. How could she have a child at her age? She, who often told people that nothing was too hard for God, had forgotten her own words. For it happened as the angels had said it would. A year later, when the sun's rays touched the mark on the tent, she gave birth to a boy, Isaac.

Abraham planted a tamarisk tree and roasted a lamb to celebrate, and there was rejoicing in the camp.

Hagar could no longer call Sarah barren. But, with Satan egging her on, she found new ways to taunt her former mistress. She went around the camp saying, "My son is the first-born. Ishmael will inherit from Abraham. Ishmael will lead the nation after Abraham, not little Isaac."

When people came and told this to Sarah, she answered calmly, "God did not tell Abraham and Hagar to found a nation. He told Abraham and Sarah to found it. Isaac, my son, will lead the nation."

Hagar's claims only annoyed Sarah. But the behavior of Hagar's son disturbed Sarah greatly. Ishmael was grown. He lived in a tent of his own and would soon marry. Yet he spent much time in Sarah's tent "playing with Isaac," as he called it. But was that roughness play? The jabs and slaps, was it play?

One night, when Sarah sat with the others around the fire, her fears worsened. Someone had begun telling the story of Cain and Abel. She knew the story. She had heard it many times. This time it had dark and worrisome tones. Cain and Abel were full brothers! Sons of the same mother! Yet Cain killed Abel.

The next morning, when Sarah saw Abraham sitting outside his tent, she went up to him and said, "Send Hagar and her son away."

Abraham did not want to do it. "She is your maid, do as you please," he said.

"You let it happen, and you must be the one to do it," Sarah said. "You heard her mock me and did not stop her. You hear her saying that Ishmael will lead the nation and do not correct her. You see Ishmael toss Isaac in the air and do not chastise him. What do you do? You leave the tent and go sit outside."

"Ishmael is my son, too," Abraham said.

Sarah had nothing to say. She left Abraham sitting outside, plunged in gloom. He remained sitting outside until darkness fell. When he rose to go in, he saw an amber cloud on the mount and he heard a voice say, "Do as Sarah says. Ishmael will found another nation. The nation of which I spoke to you, that nation you will found with Sarah."

The next morning, Abraham prepared food and water for Hagar and Ishmael. He accompanied them a little way, then parted with them.

On his way back, his foot struck an object. He bent and picked it up. And what was it? The copy of the Emerald Book of Secrets that the angel Raziel had given to Noah, which Noah had hidden after the Flood.

The book was alive. It spoke of recent events, and others soon to come. As Prince Metatron wrote in heaven's copy of the book, the writing also appeared in the hidden copy.

CHAPTER 20
Satan Schemes

Satan had managed to create strife in the tents of the Servants of God, but little more. He had failed in his main effort, to stir up the evil urge in Abraham and Sarah. They would do nothing to offend God. He could not swerve them from the path of goodness.

But as he watched Isaac grow and saw the love Abraham and Sarah had for the boy, he formed a new plan. To carry it out he would have to speak to God. That was possible, but a delicate matter. Possible, because a Fallen Angel may ask to speak with God. A delicate matter, because his two greatest enemies were in charge of the Gate for Fallen Angels—Prince Metatron and angel Raziel. Prince Metatron was certain to deny his request. Angel Raziel might be easier to persuade.

Satan recited code words that reached Raziel's ears.

"Speak," she said.

"Good angel Raziel," he began.

Raziel, recognizing his detested voice, interrupted, "'Good angel Raziel,' is it?" she said. "Good I am, and do not need you to tell me so. What do you want?"

"I wish to speak to the Holy One," Satan said.

"Blasphemer!" she said. "Only holy beings may use that name."

Satan had forgotten. He rephrased his request. "May I speak to the almighty God?" he said.

"On what subject?"

"Abraham and Sarah."

Raziel could not refuse, not when the subject was Abraham and Sarah. Turning to the Holy Curtain, she placed Satan's request before the Holy One.

"He may speak from the border," the Holy One said.

At a signal from Raziel, the Gate for Fallen Angels swung open and a sucking wind rushed to the edge of a dark, narrow, smoky tunnel and pulled Satan up, up, up, toward the seventh heaven.

As he rose, Satan could hear the sweet voices in the Heavenly Choir singing.

> When we sing your praises
> the taste in our mouths
> is sweeter than honey
> more pleasing than wine.

As a Fallen Angel, Satan could not cry. Tears are a gift of God. They relieve sadness and let gladness have its way. But so piercingly sweet was the singing, his eyes misted over.

His head snapped back as he arrived at the border.

"Speak from there," said Prince Metatron.

Satan trembled. The rays of Glory barely reached the border. They were palest there. But even there, even so far from the Holy Curtain, he felt the edges of joy.

"I miss heaven, God," he said.

The listening angels knew Satan had spoken truly. A false word spoken in heaven set off a loud metallic clang.

"You have come about my servants, Abraham and Sarah?" God said.

Satan remembered the metallic clang. He told himself to be careful. On earth, he lied freely. He did not want to slip into a lie out of habit. He would answer a question with a question. A question, strictly speaking, could not be a lie.

"You call them your servants," he said. "And so they are. But how long will they remain so?"

"Speak plainly," God said.

"They have taught their followers to worship you, and the followers do so. But when Abraham and Sarah look away, some go outside the camp to worship idols."

No clang. It was true.

"They work to correct the situation," the Holy One said.

"They try," Satan said.

"But . . . ?"

"They are not firm; they do not punish."

No clang. Also true.

"But they themselves are loyal to me," the Holy One said.

"They speak of your greatness. They teach your love of goodness, of justice, mercy. They sacrifice to you—"

"Then what have you come to say?" God said.

"I wonder if they will remain loyal to you," Satan said.

"Explain yourself," said the Holy One.

"You have given them cattle and flocks and made them wealthy. You have given them the desire of their hearts—a son in their old age."

"That is so," the Holy One said.

"There is nothing left for them to want," Satan said.

"That is not a worry."

"Not for them," Satan said. "But if they have everything, what do they need you for? They might turn away from you and worship stars again."

Satan's deviousness was known in heaven.

"They will always worship me," God said.

"Humans have disappointed you before."

No clang.

"Abraham and Sarah will always do whatever I ask," God said. "Even sacrifice Isaac to me, if I asked it."

Satan tried to hide his pleasure. The very words he had hoped to hear! "There is only one way to find out if they will," he said, trying to sound nonchalant. "Test them."

The sucking wind yanked Satan away from the border and thrust him down the dark, narrow, smoky tunnel, tossing and bumping him from side to side along the way. It was a rude journey. But Satan was too satisfied with himself to care.

CHAPTER 21
Sarah Sees Another Meaning

The Holy One knew Abraham and Sarah loved him. He knew they were steadfast and loyal. He had faith in them. Yet he did test them.

"Abraham," he said, "bring your son Isaac to Moriah, to one of the mounts, and offer him there for a burnt offering."

Abraham would do it. He would do whatever God asked. But the command puzzled him. God detested child sacrifice. Abraham did not raise the question. He could not understand God's ways. God was too great, too different, for that. But about Moriah, a hilly place with many mounts, he did raise a question.

"On which mount shall I take my son Isaac?" he said.

"You will see my Glory descending on that one," God said.

While Abraham had withheld the question from God, he spoke to Sarah about what troubled him. "Why would God, who hates child sacrifice, ask this?" he said to her.

Sarah and he had read the future in the Emerald Book of Secrets. The book said Isaac and Rebecca would be the next leaders of God's nation. She reminded him of this. And she said, "Repeat again God's words to me."

Abraham did so.

"I see a hidden meaning in the words," she said.

"I am listening," Abraham said.

"We have banned child sacrifice, but some still practice it in secret," she said.

The thought saddened Abraham. "And then they tell us that the child has wandered off, disappeared," he said.

"They do not take the ban seriously," Sarah said.

"You were speaking of a hidden meaning—?"

"The word *Moriah* means instruction," Sarah said. "That tells me the journey is intended to teach something."

The thought had the ring of truth for Abraham. He became busy saddling his donkey and sent a servant to bring Isaac.

The boy came running. "Here I am, Father."

"Prepare yourself for a journey," Abraham said as he filled water skins to take.

The thought of a journey excited Isaac, and he hurried off to wash and make himself ready.

"Tell the two burly boys they will be leaving with Abraham," Sarah called after him.

"Why them?" Abraham said. "Boaz and Efriyim usually accompany me."

"These two are just as able to fight off bandits if any appear," Sarah said. "They are also good storytellers and will entertain Isaac along the way."

"That they are," Abraham said, putting the water skins into the donkey's side pocket.

"The best reason for taking them," Sarah said, "is their gossipy natures. They will make known the details of the journey."

She went in and returned with lentil cakes and bread and put them into the donkey's second pocket. As Abraham tucked a knife and stones to make fire into his sash, Sarah noticed people standing in the doors of their tents, watching.

"Take also wood," she said.

"I will find wood along the way," Abraham said.

"With wood, you will have everything for a sacrifice," she said. "Let the people see it and wonder why you go outside the camp to sacrifice. They will be impatient for the return of the burly boys and the news they bring."

Abraham's party was ready to leave the camp. The burly boys were on hand. A servant had strapped wood to the donkey's back. Sarah held Isaac in a long embrace and waited to see him go. The eyes of the followers were on them as they left the camp.

They journeyed for two days, stopping to sleep nights in camps where Abraham was known, and on the third day, they arrived in Moriah.

"It is hilly, Father," Isaac said, looking about. "Different from our desert home."

Abraham nodded, walking on, watching the hilltops, looking for a sign. Then he saw it. No one else saw it, only he did.

"Let us stop here," he said.

The others had seen only a footpath leading up to a thicket and in a clearing at the top, a large stone for an altar. Abraham had seen more. He had seen the Shekina, the amber cloud, lower herself onto the mount.

Abraham took the wood from the donkey's back and gave some to Isaac to carry. And he said to the burly boys, "I will go up with Isaac to sacrifice. You wait here with the donkey."

The burly boys squatted, settling down to wait with the donkey. They were

Only Abraham could see the Shekina and amber cloud.

mystified, watching Abraham go up with the boy. Abraham had come here to sacrifice. But where was the lamb?

At the top of the mount, as Abraham arranged wood on the stone for a fire, Isaac also wondered about the sacrifice.

"Father," he said, "I see wood. I see stones to make fire. I see the knife. But where is the lamb for sacrifice?"

Abraham knelt and took the boy in his arms. "Do you love God?" he said.

"With all my heart," Isaac said.

"If God asked you to sacrifice yourself to him, what would you do?"

"I would not refuse," he said.

"God has asked this of you," Abraham said.

"I will do whatever God asks," Isaac said. He added, a moment later, "I am only human, Father. I might run away when I see the knife coming. Bind me to hold me down."

Abraham reached into the thicket, pulled out two sinewy vines, and bound Isaac's hands and feet.

Below, the burly boys gasped. Abraham was their beloved leader. He preached against child sacrifice. Yet he was about to sacrifice his son! They watched, stupefied, as Abraham raised his knife over the boy. They leapt to their feet when a moment later they heard a heavenly voice say, "Abraham, do not touch the boy. God hates human sacrifice."

They heard a crash and saw a ram stumble into the thicket and become tangled up in the vines. And they could hear Abraham say to Isaac, "God has provided a sacrifice for himself."

Abraham unbound his son's hands and feet. And he and the lad prepared the lamb for sacrifice and offered it up to God. The burly boys stared at them when they came down.

"We saw it," said one, wide-eyed.

"The voice, we heard it," said the other.

Abraham remembered Sarah's words, that the journey was intended to teach and that the boys had a gossipy nature. "Tell it," he said, and lifted Isaac onto the donkey's back.

Facing the mount, he said, "I name this place *Adonoy-Yireh*. God sees and is seen here." And turning to Isaac, he said, "I add to the word *Yireh* the word *shalem*— whole and peace. For you have remained whole, and my heart is at peace."

Gladness rippled through heaven.

Raziel said to the Holy One, "Now all the earth will know that you hate child sacrifice, beloved."

"And every angel will now know that Abraham and Sarah love me," the Holy One said.

Angel laughter sparkled through heaven.

The angels understood that his words were meant not for them but for Satan.

Over time, a city grew around Mount Moriah. To this day it bears the name that Abraham gave it—*Yiru-shalem*—Jerusalem.

NOTES AND REFERENCES

Below are Bible references and, under the heading *From Legend*, elements of Midrash, commentary, and legend on which the stories in this book are based.
Chapter titles are Midrashim, Bible commentary, or legend.
The narrative thread and dialogue are the author's.
Angel love songs are adapted from Psalms and from Jewish prayers.

INTRODUCTION

From the Bible:

Man cannot know God's work. Ecclesiastes 3:11. / He stretched out the heavens as a curtain. Isaiah 40:22. / Love your neighbor as yourself. Leviticus 19:18. / His tender mercies are over all his works. Psalm 145:9. / Be thoughtful of the stranger, eyes for the blind. Job 29:15. / Heaven is my throne. Isaiah 66:1. / [Heaven] was full of the brightness of the Lord's Glory. Ezekiel 10:4. / Is not my word . . . like a hammer? Jeremiah 23:29.

From Legend:

Turn it and turn it . . . for everything is in it. / The secrets of heaven belong to God. / "Holy One," a name for God. / God was talking to the angels. / Goodness is loving kindness, a rule of Jewish ethics./Do not do to others what you would not have them do to you.

CHAPTER 1/GOD CREATED THE ANGELS ON THE SECOND DAY
From the Bible:

Darkness was upon the face of the deep; and the spirit [this word in Hebrew is feminine] of God hovered over the face of the waters. Genesis 1:2./A thousand years in your [God's] sight are but as yesterday when it is past. Psalm 90:4./The whole world is full of his Glory. Isaiah 6:3./None shall see me and live. Exodus 33:20./You set boundaries. Psalm 104:9./Heaven is my throne and the earth my footstool. Isaiah 66:1./Sing unto the Lord, all the earth. Psalm 96:1./There is Leviathan. Psalm 104:26./God, riding through heaven to help you. Deuteronomy 33:26./ . . . all that is in heaven and earth is [God's]. I Chronicles 29:11.

Angels: . . . feet like a calf's and hands under the wings. Ezekiel 1:7–8./ . . . seraphim had six wings; with two they cover their face. Isaiah 6:2./And all the angels shouted [sang praises] for joy. Job 38:7./So he [the angel Gabriel] came near where I stood. Daniel 8:17./I will send an angel before you. Exodus 33:2.

From Legend:

Angels sing praises to God from the beginning of time./The seven heavens./The Holy Curtain./Width of heaven, depth of sea./Leviathan, Ziz, Behemoth./Where the earth kisses heaven./In Jewish mystical literature, angel Raziel, whose name means Hears God's secrets, sits outside the Holy Curtain./The choir consists of myriads of angel singers and musicians.

CHAPTER 2 / THE ANGELS ARE JEALOUS

From the Bible:

Let us make man in our image. Genesis 1:26–27. / What is man that you should be mindful of him? Psalm 8:5. [This psalm generates stories about jealous angels and angels arguing with God.] / When pride comes, then comes shame. Proverbs 11:2. / The Lord by wisdom founded the earth. Proverbs 3:19. / The earth is the Lord's and the fullness thereof. Psalm 24:1. / Male and female created he them. Genesis 1:27; 5:2. / God . . . breathed life into his nostrils. Genesis 2:7. / The sound of stringed instruments. Psalm 92:4.

Satan: came also . . . to incite God against Job. Job 2:1. / Standing at his right to accuse him. Zechariah 3:1. / Incited David to number Israel. I Chronicles 21:1.

From Legend:

Satan: Based on the above biblical passages, he is a former good angel, the angel who did not [respect] the new creation [humans], an accuser of humans before God. He is also the evil urge, the snake in the garden, the angel of death.

Female angels in this book are based as well on sages' comments: He created Adam as an androgyne [a man-woman]. / Cherubim [a type of angel] . . . appear as men, women, spirits, angels.

A star is superior. / Oh, you fools in the world! An expression. / At night, angels sing. By day, Israel [humans] should. / Bring red, black, white and yellow dust [to prevent future quarrels]. / A soul was added [to the human creation]. / Skin of Glory, a sort of garment of light, like a piece of smoke, like the glow of a torch. / Everything is in God's hands except the fear of God.

From Jewish Teachings about God:

There is one God who is God in heaven and on earth./God has no substance and cannot be seen./God as Creator is the root of the Jewish faith./He is made of, but not limited to, the spiritual qualities described in Exodus 34:6, "kind, merciful, gracious, full of patience, goodness, truth."/Plus two more, intelligence and understanding./Likeness of God means a spiritual likeness, possessing God's qualities.

El is another name for God. Archangels' names in Hebrew reflect their devotion to God. Michael—There is no one like God. Gabriel—Man of God. Raphael—God heals. Uriel—God is my light.

CHAPTER 3 / SATAN IS CAST OUT OF HEAVEN
From the Bible:

Stories of Fallen Angels grow out of Genesis 6:1–4.

From Legend:

Satan inciting the angels, the author's invention./Mount Hermon. The name carries the Hebrew word *hrm*, excommunication.

CHAPTER 4 / WHAT DOES THE WORLD YET LACK? ONLY REST
From the Bible:

The garden of Eden. Genesis 2:8./The jeweled pathways of the garden. Ezekiel 28:13./The heaven and the earth were finished. Genesis 2:1./He rested on the seventh day . . . and blessed it. Genesis 2:2–3./The Creator does not faint or grow weary. Isaiah 40:28./Let the Lord rejoice in his works. Psalm 104:31./My beloved is mine and I am his. Song of Songs 2:16./Holy, Holy, Holy is God who made the world. Isaiah 6:3.

From Legend:

Adam and Eve fear the darkness./The Holy One rests out of gladness./Ministering angels came down./Jews usher in the Sabbath singing to invisible angels who come down to earth: "Peace be yours, ministering angels, messengers of the Most High, the supreme king of kings, holy and blessed is he."/Adam must have sung when he beheld the works of nature.

CHAPTER 5/THE SHEKINA, GOD'S FEMALE SIDE AND HIS EARTH PRESENCE

From the Bible:

Adam and Eve in the garden. Genesis 2:5./Can anyone hide . . . that I shall not see him? Jeremiah 23:24./God is sorry he made Adam and Eve. Genesis 6:7.

The Shekina, God's earth presence: derives from: Let them make me [God] a sanctuary, that I may dwell among them. Exodus 25:8./I will walk among you and be your God. Leviticus 26:12./I will be the glory in the midst of her [of Jerusalem]. Zechariah 2:9./The earth shone with God's Glory. Ezekiel 43:2./A slanderer shall not be established in the earth. Psalm 140:12.

From Legend:

Serpent was a sort of camel./The fruit was perhaps fig or pomegranate. It was not named, to keep it from becoming hated./ The Serpent ate of it./God ate of it, to know how to make the world./The color of Glory is amber./God wants to see mercy mixed with justice./God made ten descents to earth in the form of the

Shekina, the first in the garden./The brilliance of the Shekina, her radiance went forth from one end of the world.

CHAPTER 6 / THE ARCHANGEL BRINGS SEEDS TO ADAM AND EVE

From the Bible:

The Cain and Abel story: Genesis 4:1–16./Can any hide . . . that I shall not see him? Jeremiah 23:24./Where shall I go? You are everywhere. Psalm 139:7–10./[Choose] life and good, or death and evil. Deuteronomy 30:15.

From Legend:

The archangel taught planting./Cain's dog, Abel's dog./Cain sacrificed left-overs./Perhaps Cain will regret his act and tell the truth./It's your fault, why didn't you stop me?/Cain was spared because there was no one to teach him./In future, whoever slays will himself be slain./ The raven teaches burial./God carries out his plan through all creatures.

CHAPTER 7 / ADAM AND EVE ALSO HAD DAUGHTERS

From the Bible:

Land of Nod. Genesis 4:16./And Eve bore . . . Seth. Genesis 4:25./And Enoch walked with God and . . . God took him. Genesis 5:24.

From Legend:

To assure the continuation of life a girl was born./Twins accounted for many births./Enoch as Metatron./There is no rivalry, no weariness among angels./You [angels] have been troublesome from the beginning./The Emerald Book of Secrets.

CHAPTER 8/LYING—GOD DID NOT CREATE THAT

From the Bible:

Man's heart is evil from youth. Genesis 8:21./The children gather firewood. Jeremiah 7:18./And the Lord repented that he had made them. Genesis 6:6./Do not allow your children to be offered up to Moloch. Leviticus 18:21.

From Legend:

Miserliness is the source of evil.

CHAPTER 9/GOOD KING METHUSELAH

From the Bible:

The Lord looked down from heaven. Psalm 14:2./And Enoch begot Methuselah. Genesis 5: 21–27./But Noah found favor in the eyes of the Lord. Genesis 6:8.

From Legend:

Naamah was Noah's wife./Noah as inventor./Methuselah as composer.

CHAPTER 10/THE EMERALD BOOK OF SECRETS, WHAT WAS IT?

From the Bible:

The story of the flood and the ark. Genesis 6:5.

From Legend:

The Emerald Book of Secrets delivered by Raziel, author's invention./There are good demons./Animal episodes.

CHAPTER 11 / SATAN ACCOMPANIES THE ARK
Scene, author's invention.

CHAPTER 12 / THE ANIMALS HAVE TO BE FED
From the Bible:

And the dove came in . . . with an olive-leaf. Genesis 8:11. / I will not again curse the ground. Genesis 8:21–22. / I establish my covenant with you. Genesis 9:9.

From Legend:

A precious stone gave light. / Animal episodes. / Olive branch from Mount of Olives. / The animals offer themselves for sacrifice.

CHAPTER 13 / SATAN'S FOLLOWERS TEAM UP WITH DEMONS
From the Bible:

The [angels] took wives. Genesis 6:2. / The [women] walking and mincing . . . and making a tinkling with their feet. Isaiah 3:16.

From Legend:

Demons are the offspring of humans and wild beasts. / They leave footprints in the morning, like a cock's.

CHAPTER 14 / NOAH'S VINE BRANCH
From the Bible:

Hatred stirs up strife. Proverbs 10:12. / And Noah planted a vineyard. Genesis 9:20. / The sons covered the nakedness of their father. Genesis 9:23.

From Legend:

Noah drank wine not in a cup, but in a bowl. / Scene of family strife invented by author.

CHAPTER 15 / A NEW CLASS OF ANGELS

From the Bible:

Some [angels] walk to and fro on earth. Zechariah 1:10. / [Nimrod] began to be mighty on earth. Genesis 10:8. / The Tower of Babel story. Genesis 11:1–9.

From Legend:

Nimrod. / Satan's disguises.

CHAPTER 16 / THE IDOL SHOP IN UR

From the Bible:

The Abraham and Sarah story. Genesis 12:1. / Hatred of Moloch. Leviticus 18:21. / God is God in heaven above and on earth below. Deuteronomy 4:39. / Lift up your eyes and see who created these things. Isaiah 40:26.

From Legend:

Terah as idol maker. / Emtelai, his wife.

CHAPTER 17 / THE EARTH WALKERS HAVE A SURPRISE

From the Bible:

He fills heaven and earth but you cannot see him. Jeremiah 23:24. / The noise of the wings of the living creatures as they touched one another. Ezekiel 3:13.

From Legend:

Selling idols. / Oh, you fool in the world, an expression.

CHAPTER 18 / ABRAHAM CONVERTS THE MEN, SARAH, THE WOMEN

From the Bible:

Do not devise evil [against your neighbor] for I hate this. Zechariah 8:17. / Ask the birds of the air. Job 12:7. / Be just, do what is lawful and what is right. Ezekiel 18:5. / I am God, there is no one else. I form the light and create darkness. Isaiah, 45:7. / Serve the Lord with gladness, come to him with singing. Psalm 100:2.

From Legend:

Woman at baths. / Idol smashing. / Do your ears hear what your mouth is saying? / The tent. / Study the miracles of the world to know the Creator. / Before, God was known to his creatures in heaven. Now I [Abraham] have made him known to his creatures on earth.

CHAPTER 19 / GOD ENTERS THE WORLD

From the Bible:

Abraham's family. Genesis 12:1. / They shall bring forth fruit in old age. Psalm 92:15. / Nothing is too hard for God. Genesis 18:14. / She is your maid, do as you please. Genesis 16:6.

From Legend:

All the earth belongs to the Holy One. / Michael, Gabriel, Rafael are named as the angels [who appear as men]. / Sarah was a seer. / Emerald Book here, author's invention.

CHAPTER 20 / SATAN SCHEMES

From the Bible:

. . . and Satan came also . . . to incite God against Job. Job 2:3.

From Legend:

Satan challenged God to test Abraham. / Tears are a gift of God.

CHAPTER 21 / SARAH SEES ANOTHER MEANING

From the Bible:

. . . turn away from your idols. Ezekiel 14:6. / The sacrifice of Isaac story. Genesis 22. / Now I know that you fear God. Genesis 22:12. / Moriah is Jerusalem. 2 Chronicles 3.1. / And he called the place Adonai-Yireh. Genesis 22:14.

From Legend:

Moriah means instruction. / A prophetic spirit was in Sarah. / Abraham recognized the cloud of Glory. / Isaac remained shalem and Abraham found peace—author invention. / All heaven now knows that Abraham loves me. / I [Abraham] have made it known that God hates child sacrifice.

BOOKS FOR FURTHER READING

For Young Readers

Cone, Molly. *Who Knows Ten? Children's Tales of the Ten Commandments*. Uri Shulevitz, illus. New York: UAHC, 1965.

Freehof, Lillian S. and Howard Schwartz. *Bible Legends: An Introduction to Midrash (Genesis)*. New York: UAHC Press, 1987.

Gellman, Marc. *Does God Have a Big Toe? Stories About Stories in the Bible*. Oscar De Mejo, illus. New York: Harper & Row, 1989.

Gerstein, Mordicai. *The Shadow of a Flying Bird: A Legend from the Kurdistani Jews*. New York: Hyperion, 1994.

Goldin, Barbara Diamond. *A Child's Book of Midrash*. Northvale, N. J. Jason Aronson, 1990.

MacGill-Callahan, Sheilah. *When Solomon Was King*. Stephen T. Johnson, illus. New York: Dial, 1995.

Rossel, Seymour. *Sefer Ha-Aggadah: The Book of Legends for Young Readers*. Judy Dick, illus. New York: UAHC Press, 1996. Volume I. Stories retold from the classic work, *Book of Legends*, translated from the Hebrew by Braude, listed above.

Schwartz, Howard and Barbara Rush. *The Diamond Tree: Jewish Tales from Around the World*. New York: HarperCollins, 1991.

Simon, Solomon and Morrison Bial, eds. *The Rabbis' Bible, Vol. 1: Torah*. New York: Behrman House, 1966. An abridged version of the first five books of the Bible with Midrashim.

For Adult Readers

Goldin, Judah. *The Living Talmud*. Selections, translated and with commentaries. New Haven, Conn: Yale University Press, 1957. New York: New American Library, 1957.

Hertz, Joseph H. *Sayings of the Fathers*, translation and commentary. New York: Behrman House, 1945. Ethical teachings.

Klagsbrun, Francine. *Voices of Wisdom: Jewish Ideals and Ethics for Everyday Living*. New York: Pantheon Books, 1980.

Patai, Raphael. *Gates to the Old City: A Book of Jewish Legends*. Northvale, N. J.: Jason Aronson, 1988.

Vilnay, Zev. *Legends of Jerusalem, The Sacred Land*. Philadelphia: Jewish Publication Society, 1973.

Bibles

The Holy Scriptures, Philadelphia: Jewish Publication Society, 1955.
Chamberlin, Roy B. and Herman Feldman. *The Dartmouth Bible, An Abridgment of the King James Version*. Sentry Edition. Boston: Houghton Mifflin, 1961.

Hertz, Joseph H. ed. *The Pentateuch and Haftorahs*: with notes and commentary. London: Soncino Press, 1978.

Plaut, W. Gunther. *The Torah, A Modern Commentary*. New York: UAHC, 1981.

Rashi's Commentary. *Pentateuch with Targum Onkelos, Haphtaroth*. Translated and annotated by Rabbi A. K. Silbermann in collaboration with Rev. M. Rosenbaum. Jerusalem and New York: Feldheim Publishers, 1985.

Books of Midrashim

Braude, William G. *The Book of Legends*, translated. Edited by Hayim Nahman Bialik and Yehoshua Hana Ravnitzky. New York: Schocken, 1992. Legends from the Talmud and Midrashim. A classic.

Freedman, Rabbi Dr. H. *Midrash Rabbah*, translated. London and Bournemouth: Soncino Press, 1951. Ten collections of Midrashim: Genesis, Exodus, Leviticus, Numbers, Deuteronomy, Ecclesiastes, Lamentations, Song of Songs, Ruth, and Esther.

Friedlander, Gerald. *The Chapters of Rabbi Eliezer the Great*, translated and annotated. New York: Sepher Hermon Press, 1981.

Ginzberg, Louis. *Legends of the Bible*. Philadelphia: Jewish Publication Society, 1978. A single, shortened version of Ginzberg's classic seven-volume work, *The Legends of the Jews*.

Goldin, Judah. *The Fathers According to Rabbi Nathan*, translated. New Haven and London: Yale University Press, 1955. An interpretation, with Herbert Danby's translation of *Chapters of the Fathers*.

ABOUT THE AUTHOR

Miriam Chaikin was born in Jerusalem and grew up in Brooklyn. She is the author of many prize-winning books of Jewish interest, including for Clarion *A Nightmare in History, Joshua in the Promised Land*, and others. She divides her time between New York City and Israel.

ABOUT THE ARTIST

David Frampton is well known for his woodcut illustrations which have appeared in many books, including *Joshua in the Promised Land, Whaling Days* by Carol Carrick (also Clarion), and *Miro in the Kingdom of the Sun* by Jane Kurtz (Houghton). He lives with his wife and their two children in New Hampshire.